LITTLE BITS

CURIOSITIES ABOUT COMPUTERS

Little Bits, Curiosities About Computers
by Víctor Romero

ISBN Hard Cover: 9798839625860
ISBN Paper Back: 9798840738023

CONTENTS

Probably, the most memorable science fiction moment is Darth Vader telling Luke Skywalker: I am your father. Why do we remember this instead of the many other events of the saga? Is it perhaps due to the surprise factor it had?

What should it be if, after a long physics class, we cannot remember the formulas, but we can perfectly remember and visualize Sir Isaac Newton suffering the fall of an apple on his head? How many physics fans love physics through this and other small anecdotes?

As humans, since ancient times when we gathered by the fire to learn from the stories of the elders, we prefer and remember amazing stories rather than any other kind of information. And Computer science can be explained as a story told around the fire, from what is a bit to quantum supremacy, including the lives of brilliant personalities such as Ada Lovelace or Grace Hopper.

Computer science can be in equal measure overwhelming or exciting. Perhaps it just depends on the way it is learned. So surely, there was a need for a book that would explain computer culture to people just beginning to approach this world and to veterans seeking to learn more about the roots of their knowledge.

With a sincere eagerness to spread enthusiasm, this book provides numerous illustrated and surprising stories, anecdotes, quotes, and folklore about computing.

Hardware

It's the hardware that makes a computer fast. It's the software that makes a fast computer go slow.

— Craig Bruce, Canadian computer scientist

WHAT IS A BIT?

When we human beings learn how to count, we use a numbering system that goes from zero to ten. This is not the result of chance. We count with the ten fingers of our hands. It is likely that if we had sixteen fingers instead of counting in decimal, we would have counted in hexadecimal.

A computer has to manage with a single finger. That is, while humans can count from zero to ten, the computer can go only from 0 to 1, so it counts in binary and represents it with whether or not there is voltage in its small internal wires.

Decimal	Binary
0	0
1	1
2	10
3	11
4	100
5	101
6	110
7	111
8	1000
9	1001
10	1010
11	1011
12	1100
13	1101
14	1110
15	1111

The use of zeros and ones to represent information dates back to 1732, when Basille Bouchon and Jean-Baptiste Falcon invented the punched card to automate looms (see Programming by punching holes, 88). But the word *bit* is much more recent. Where does it come from?

In 1947, John Tukey, a mathematician who had a spectacular career while working at Bell labs, contracted the words *binary digit* into bit in an internal memorandum. A year later, Claude E. Shannon, the considered father of information theory, made the term popular by using it in one of his publications.

> *There are only 10 types of people in the world: those who understand binary and those who don't.*
>
> *— Math joke*

THE BYTE AND THE WORD

Early computers worked with groups of bits called words that were ideally sized to represent numbers.

For scientists in the early days of computing, everything revolved around numbers and calculations. Therefore, the word was the most important thing. Representing characters with words was secondary and inefficient. In many systems, a word had 16 bits, and often no more than 6 bits were used to represent a character, so 10 bits were wasted for each. This occurred in times when RAM was a very precious commodity.

It was sometime later when the engineer Werner Buchholz of the legendary company IBM named the group of bits necessary to encode a character as byte (joking with a bigger bit) and began to design computers that were good at dealing with characters and dealing with numbers. The byte did not always have precisely eight bits, but today this amount is widely considered standardized.

Did you know?

Despite the fact the byte is the unit of measurement par excellence in modern computing, the word still has a small place that does not seem to lose at all.

In video game consoles and computers, a number of bits are usually given to define their architecture: 8 bits, 16 bits, 32 bits, 64 bits, etc. This mysterious number refers to the size of your word and, therefore, the size and accuracy of the numbers it can handle.

A VERY REAL BUG

We often use the term bug to refer to software or hardware errors. It has become a widespread term and even has derivatives such as debug, which is the process of finding and eliminating these errors, or the adjective buggy, reserved for programs with many errors.

The first time the term was recorded as a computer bug was exactly at 3:45 pm on September 9, 1947. A team of engineers, including the famous Grace Hopper (see programming for everyone, 81), was informed of an error in an electromagnetic relay.

In relay 70 of Panel F of the Aiken Harvard Mark II calculator, a moth was found as the origin of the problem. The moth was attached with adhesive tape in the log with the comment: *First actual case of bug being found.* Unfortunately, they left the window open, which was enough to attract the moth to the machine's lights and heat.

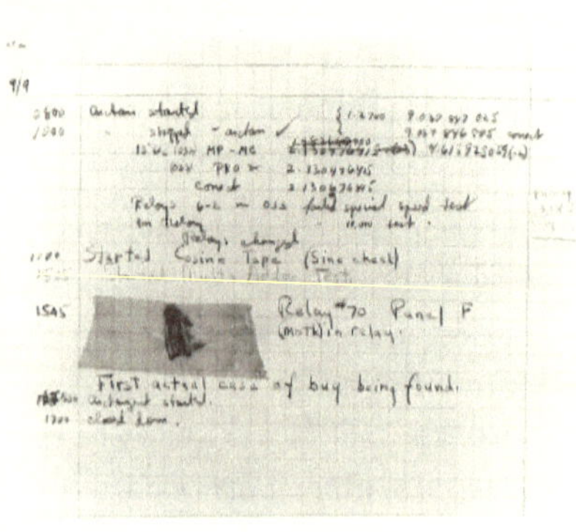

> *If debugging is the process of removing software bugs, then programming should be the process of putting them in.*
>
> — *Edger Dijkstra, computer scientist from the Netherlands*

However, this was not the first bug case found, but the first computer-related bug case found. The first written reference is from 1843, in which the famous inventor Thomas Alva Edison writes in a letter to William Orton, the president of Western Union: *You were partly right, I found a bug in my device, but not exactly in the phone.*

Don't miss it

The log in which the moth is found is today part of the Smithsonian National Museum of American History collection. Although it is usually not exhibited, sometimes it appears in temporary exhibitions.

BE MY COMPETITOR

It's not surprising to see the two most prominent manufacturers of desktop and laptop CPUs, Intel and AMD, competing fiercely for the market. But would it be surprising that AMD does it thanks to Intel?

In 1975 AMD was just a small company that managed to clone Intel's successful 8080 microprocessor. However, legally speaking, cloning was a highly complex activity. As a result, AMD was likely to be in for a tortuous future plagued by court visits, just as it was for the other companies that ventured out to do so like Cyrix.

On the other hand, it is not necessary to present the IBM PC, the personal computer that served as the basis for most personal computing for decades and still does so in many ways.

In 1982 IBM contemplated the possibility of using Intel's 8080 processor for the new design they had in hand, their IBM PC. However, the blue giant had internal rules that used to impose on its suppliers: they would only buy chips with at least two suppliers (to protect themselves in case of suppliers' bankruptcy).

The IBM PC business seemed to be (and indeed was) very important, and Intel needed someone to compete with itself to access it. Thus, in 1982, Intel licensed its intellectual property to AMD, which became the second largest supplier, effectively creating its most significant competitor.

THE FIRST WEBCAM

In 1991, the University of Cambridge's computer department used the same fuel to innovate that we use today: caffeine.

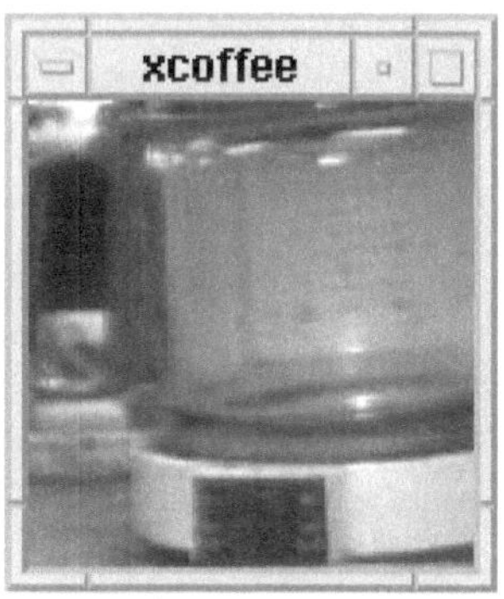

The problem was that the coffee maker they used was in the now famous Trojan room, while the researchers were spread over other rooms and floors. As a result, it was common to take a long walk to the cafeteria only to find no coffee left.

To solve this vital problem, researchers James Quentin Stafford-Frase (the original author of the VNC for Windows) and Paul Jardetzky wrote a small client-server program that allowed researchers to view the coffee maker from any terminal in the laboratory.

Just a couple of years later, web browsers began to be able to show images, and that's when they changed the program so that only a browser was needed to see what was behind the camera through the web, thus giving birth to the first webcam.

> *One of the things that's very, very important in computer science research is a regular and dependable flow of caffeine.*
>
> *— Dr Quentin Stafford-Fraser, computer scientist*

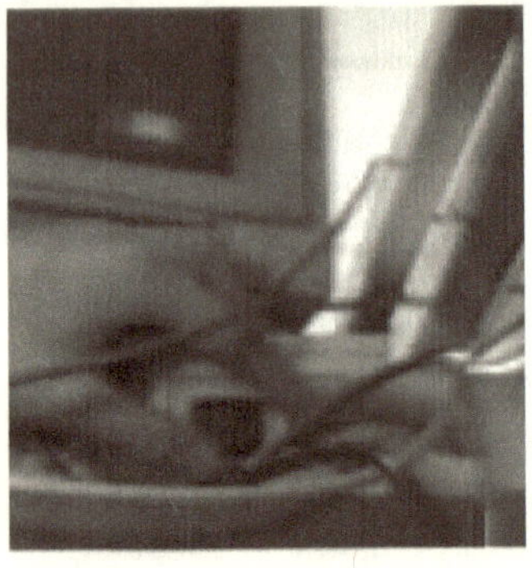

The camera was trendy for years until when the laboratories changed facilities. The last image was retransmitted with a tragic end: a hand on top of a mouse about to turn off the server.

And what about the coffee pot? It was auctioned on eBay to the German news website Spiegel Online. It was refurbished and later loaned permanently to the Heinz Nixdorf MuseumsForum in Paderborn.

THE BEST-SELLING COMPUTER IN HISTORY

What is the best-selling computer in history? Many would likely think it is an IBM PC or perhaps some Apple model.

To know which, according to the Guinness Book of Records, is the best-selling computer in history is necessary to go back to the early '80s. Back then, a personal computer cost a large sum of money, and most households couldn't afford one.

Jack Tramiel was a Polish-born Jewish businessman. He arrived rescued by the infantry to the United States from no other place than the Auschwitz concentration camp, where he was examined and even elected to a working group by Dr. Mengele. Jack founded the legendary Commodore company and reflected its spirit in the famous phrase: *We design for the masses, not for the classes.*

The result of this design philosophy was the Commodore 64. Which later earned him the nickname of the anti-Steve Jobs for his disinterest in design and his interest in low cost. However, unlike Steve Jobs, his enormous contribution to the standardization and democratization of computers in homes has yet to be adequately recognized.

> *When I was 9, my parents gave me a Commodore 64, which was fun. At the time, the opportunity to program your own computer was easier than it is today. Today there are significantly larger barriers because of the complexity built into computing.*
>
> — *Sergey Brin, cofounder of Google LLC*

THE DOG WHO DESIGNED COMPUTERS

In the early '80s, Jay Miner and other Atari employees left the company fed up with management. They created a new project called Lorraine in the company Hi-Toro.

One of the critical factors that led Jay to work for Hi-Toro was that he was allowed to take his dog, Mitchy, to work. Jay said in an interview that the fact that Mitchy was there made the company more accepting of the unique personalities of the engineers they hired, some of whom were going to work with purple tights and pink bunny sandals.

Mitchy was so beloved in the company that she even had a security pass that Al Acorn, the designer of the video game Pong, got for her.

The Lorraine project and the Hi-Toro company may not be too well known by those names. But both the project and the company were renamed Amiga. A word whose sound still makes veteran fans from all over the world sigh.

The first units of the Amiga 1000 had engraved the signatures of all those who participated in its design. And this includes, of course, Mitchy's footprint, the dog recognized as an influence on the design of a computer.

Quantum supremacy

Oren Harari, a business professor at the University of San Francisco and author of numerous business administration books, said: *Electric light does not come from the continuous improvement of candles.*

Putting some limit on how much the candle can be improved, Intel co-founder Gordon E. Moore said in 2005 that his famous law, Moore's law, by which every two years the number of transistors in a microprocessor would be doubled, cannot go on forever. He expected that it would only work for 10 or 20 more years.

It seems almost evident that in the example of the light bulb and the candle, the computers based on quantum mechanics are the new light bulb, and the classic computers are the candle. This is because quantum computers, instead of bits of zeros and ones, have qubits whose value can be between zero and one. Moreover, these qubits are processed with remarkable parallelism using quantum gates. As a result, they can perform operations that no classical computer could perform in a reasonable time (and sometimes, reasonable means in less time than the universe's age).

> *Nature isn't classical, dammit, and if you want to make a simulation of nature, you'd better make it quantum mechanical.*
>
> — *Richard Feynman, American theoretical physicist*

Hardware

When a quantum computer is created that can perform a problem that cannot be computed with a classical supercomputer, it is said that quantum supremacy will be achieved. Until relatively recently, this was a purely theoretical concept, but in 2019 Google claimed to have achieved quantum supremacy. Although this announcement has been controversial and IBM has even questioned it.

This field of science is undoubtedly exciting, but at the moment, quantum computers are based on superconductors that have to work at temperatures close to absolute zero, so don't expect to have them at home too soon.

KEYBOARDS SLOW DOWN

You probably have a keyboard nearby right now. If you had it and your language uses Latin characters, the first row of letters below the numbers and to the right of the tab may spell QWERTY (or perhaps QUERTZ depending on your country). These six letters give the name to the most widely used Latin character keyboard layout today.

QWERTY was not always predominant. In the days of typewriters, each manufacturer chose its key layout. Often these were simply sorted in alphabetical order.

These layouts created problems since on typewriters, all type-holder levers hit in the center, and therefore there was a good chance that two levers would get stuck if they were close and used one after the other often.

To avoid these jams, American inventor and politician Christopher L. Sholes invented a key layout that put the most commonly used keys as far away from the center of the keyboard as possible.

Although at the time of its invention, this distribution made the writer faster by dealing with fewer jams. Today, having been the distribution transferred to computer keyboards, where jams are not possible, QUERTY has lost its raison d'être.

> *The Macintosh uses an experimental pointing device called a mouse. There is no evidence that anyone wants to use those things.*
>
> — *John C. Dvorak, american columnist*

Over the years, other keyboard layouts have been designed to optimize typing. Perhaps the most famous of the distributions is the Dvorak, invented in 1936 by August Dvorak. It was carefully designed to improve typing speed, reduce mistakes and unnecessary finger movements.

In Dvorak, the most common letters are located in the middle row, with the consonants on the right and the vowels on the left. 70% of the writing is done in the middle row, while in QWERTY, this only reaches 32%.

In QUERTY, interestingly, the longest word in the English dictionary that can be written only with the top row of letters is *typewriter*. So is this an Easter egg (see easter eggs, 28) that Mr. Sholes left us?

THE OSBORNE EFFECT

In 1981 the Osborne company had immense success with its transportable computer (it was not a laptop like today, it was instead a kind of suitcase the size of a current semi-tower), the Osborne 1. The success was such that the company grew from two people to more than three thousand in months.

Two years later, the prototype of what in the future would be the next model, the much-improved Osborne Executive, was shown to the specialized press. The press received the request not to publish anything until later. Somehow, the word spread, and neither distributors nor merchants wanted the Osborne 1 anymore because they thought the Osborne Executive would soon be released.

Sales of the Osborne 1 dropped virtually to zero for months. The company tried to lower prices and carry out education campaigns indicating that the 1 and the executive were not real competitors but products for different types of customers. Unfortunately, sales did not pick up, and the company went inexorably bankrupt in September of the same year.

It is not the only time that something like this has happened. Famous examples of the so-called Osborne effect would be the dramatic drop in TV sales in the early '90s because it was expected that high-definition television would come out, which would still take almost ten more years to arrive. It also happened with Sega by prematurely announcing the Dreamcast, which eclipsed its Saturn causing Sega to stop making video game consoles forever.

THE MAGIC/MORE MAGIC SWITCH

One of the most famous buttons in computing history is the magic/more magic button. The story comes to us through the famous Jargon file. A file that, since 1975, has served to define the less formal computer science slang. However, it is said that its origin dates even earlier by including terminology from the Tech Model Railroad Club dating back to at least the '50s. The file also contains stories of hacker folklore, probably the most famous being the switch in question.

It tells us what happened to Guy L. Steele, the original author of the jargon file, who, while one day reviewing an MIT PDP-10 computer, found a switch stuck to the frame of the structure with an unprofessional appearance. Of course, in those times of large computers that occupied rooms, no switches were touched without perfectly knowing what it did, but that button was not labeled most descriptively. It only had written: *magic* and *more magic* in their respective positions.

Looking closely at the switch, he could see that only one cable reached it, but unfortunately the cable was lost in the tangle that penetrated the inside of the computer. Even so, a switch with a single cable is simply useless. It cannot do anything at all, so being clear that that button was nothing more than a bad joke of some engineer, he decided to activate it. The computer crashed ipso-facto. He justified it as a coincidence, but just in case, before restarting the computer, he left the magic/more magic switch as it was.

A year later, Guy told the story to another engineer who immediately doubted his sanity. Guy showed the switch to the engineer. He inspected the switch, saw that only one wire was connected, and, full of confidence, decided to change its position. Unfortunately, the computer immediately crashed again.

At that point, they needed the cavalry, so they went looking for the veteran MIT engineer, Richard Greenblatt, who inspected the switch and came to the same conclusion, but this time, he cut the wire and took out the switch with some pliers. They restarted the computer, and it has worked fine ever since.

It is not yet clear what made that switch exactly behave like that. However, a 1994 explanation suggests that the switch's body was possibly contacting the ground. When using the switch, there was some potential difference between the ground and the cable that was enough to create problems.

Guy tells in the Jargon file that he still keeps the switch in his basement and that, as superstitious as it may seem, he prefers to keep it in the more magic position just in case.

THE COLOR OF A COMPUTER

Asking a computer user today what a computer's color is does not make much sense. Some would answer black, others gray, aluminum, or white. Some computers will even be limited editions with prints of well-known characters from movies or comics.

Newer users will find it surprising to hear that there was a time when computers were hopelessly beige or, being more specific, Pantone 14-1118 TPX. There were slight variations such as broken white or raw. However, that did not save the computers of that time from being nicknamed *beige boxes*.

Another probably surprising fact is to whom we owe the innovation of starting to use beige color in computers. If we were to ask who might be to blame in a survey, a wide range of suspects would appear, from IBM to Dell, and if we asked which company was our savior, we would often say Apple. Ironies of history!

In 1977 the Apple II was presented, one of the first to use a glorious beige color (although they called it putty), a novelty in the world of personal computers. There were some previous examples of beige on computers but without the relevance and influence of the Apple II. Other brands that introduced successful computers the same year were the Radio Shack TRS-80, silver, and the Commodore PET, white.

Most personal computers before these were handcrafted by hobbyists and used to be wood-colored like the Apple I, the predecessor of the Apple II. So beige was certainly something that was perceived as novel as well as neutral enough to fit into any home. On the side of the big business computers, there was a wide range of colors: blacks, oranges, blues, reds, etc., but these used to be in rooms dedicated to them.

While this color was initially very well accepted, nothing seemed to indicate that it would become the only standard for so long. However, countries were looking ahead in ways that would be very influential.

Post-war Germany was very open to new ideas. It had developed concepts such as the bürolandschaft, a new, much more organic way of organizing offices that took a step forward regarding safety in the working environment.

According to the book ThinkPad: A different shade blue (Debora A. Dell and J. Gerry Pardy). Based on already obsolete scientific studies,

Germany ruled that reflections in office supplies were bad for workers and that they must have light colors. It is often claimed that this idea may have originated in reflections happening in the chrome parts of some typewriters.

This legislation found its way to reach other countries in Europe, and the global economy of scale did what could be expected since the cheapest thing was to manufacture in a single color for everyone, and for many years this color was beige.

Once again, contrary to what our instincts might tell us, to save us from beige came no other than IBM, the fathers of the PC. While looking for unique hallmarks for their famous laptops, the Think-Pads, they decided to use the iconic black of this product line. After much dealing with Germany, they managed to convince them to allow them to sell it there, but there was a condition: in their manual, they had to include a note saying that they were not suitable for use in the office.

While it is true that there was some other computer before the ThinkPad of a different color than beige, such as the gray series of Apple PowerBooks, the Apple II is usually considered as the initiator of beige due to the level of influence on others. At the same time, the Thinkpad is usually considered the computer that changed the trend due to its impact on the rest of the manufacturers.

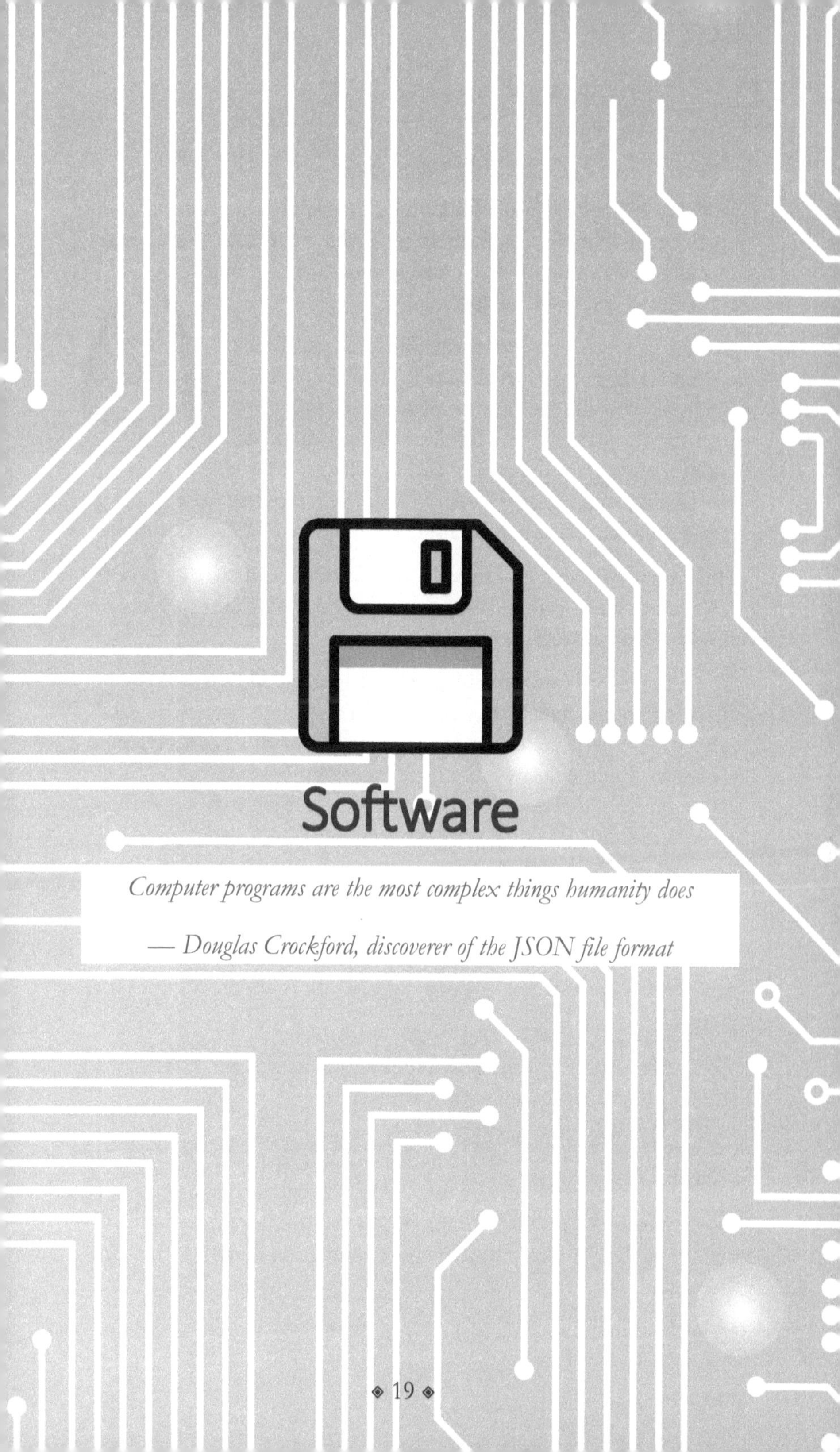

Software

Computer programs are the most complex things humanity does

— Douglas Crockford, discoverer of the JSON file format

FREE SOFTWARE

In the late '70s, MIT's artificial intelligence lab had a printer that got stuck often. The then team member Richard Stallman modified the printer's software to send an email to the team notifying it that it needed to be unclogged.

The lab got a new printer sometime later, but Richard found that times had changed. The industry had finally learned the importance of software and now protected it physically and legally. So, when Richard asked for access to the printer code to modify it for the laboratory's needs, he received a legal response asking him to sign a non-disclosure agreement that he understood as unacceptable.

He decided to resign and start the project of developing a completely free and open operating system called GNU. With this project began the free software movement.

The relationship between software and source code needs to be understood to understand free software. The source code of the software can be explained by making an analogy with a cooking recipe, where the code would be the recipe and the software would be the prepared dish; the caveat is that in this case, it is extremely difficult to get the recipe just by tasting the dish.

On free software, Richard Stallman described four rights that users would have (of which the first three require access to the source code, the recipe in our analogy):

⌨ The freedom to run the program as you wish, for any purpose (**use**).

⌨ The freedom to study how the program works, and change it so it does your computing as you wish (**study**).

⌨ The freedom to redistribute copies so you can help your neighbor (**distribution**).

⌨ The freedom to improve the program and make those improvements public to others so that the whole community benefits (**improves**).

The success of free software has been overwhelming in numerous areas of computing. Every day millions of people use free software. Android is partially open source. IOS (the iPhone operating system) runs on an open-source kernel. The operating system of the overwhelming majority of cloud services is GNU/Linux (note that GNU/Linux is the Linux kernel and GNU utilities, that is, the project started by Richard Stallman).

> *Software is like sex: it's better when it's free.*
>
> *— Linus Torvalds, Creator of Linux*

Open-source projects are often exemplary when it comes to humanity's collaborative efforts. These are usually programmers who, in their free time (although this does not always have to be the case), selflessly dedicate hours to work with other programmers to create software. Participating in these projects is the best learning tool programmers have had in recent decades, and its influence on our society is immeasurable.

THE PROBLEM OF THE YEAR 2000

Making the most of every byte has always been a source of pride for engineers, but at the dawn of computer science, it was more than just a preference; it was a necessity. RAM was a truly precious commodity.

It was because of this economy in the use of RAM and possibly because of a lack of awareness of how long-lived a program could become that often in programs written before the year 2000. Two digits were used instead of four to represent a year; e.g., instead of 1999, 99 was used.

A person's age was calculated by subtracting the birth year's last two digits from the current year's last two digits. For instance, to know the age of someone born in the year 79 in the year 99 was simple, 20 years. However, if we tried to make that calculation in 2000, we would have an age of -79.

The problems of the year 2000 did not end with the double figure. In 1578, Jesuit monks and some scientists at the University of Salamanca demonstrated an exquisite capacity for foresight by developing, without software or electronics, the sophisticated calendar we use today, the Gregorian calendar.

The Gregorian calendar is so far-sighted that it adds an extra leap year each secular year, the last of each century (i.e., those ending in 00) in case they are divisible by 400. If we put this in perspective, we could say that several centuries ago, monks and scientists calculated a calendar that would not deviate several centuries later in time. This, of course, was not taken into account by many of the programmers of the late twentieth century, despite the technology and information they had at their disposal, making the risks of the year 2000 not only at the beginning of the year but also at the end of February.

The press announced if the problem of the year 2000 were not remedied, from ATMs giving free money to trains that would collide, among other types of tragedies. It is estimated that approximately US$300 billion (without adjusting for inflation) was invested in preparing for the year 2000.

On 1 January 2000, l'école centrale de Nantes welcomed its students on 1 January 1900. Like this one, small mistakes occurred worldwide, but fortunately and thanks to foresight, there were no significant incidents to regret.

> *The lawyers and journalists are having a really bad day. The journalists have nothing to write and lawyers have no one to sue.*
>
> *— Dick Hudson, CIO de Global Marine Inc.*

In the year 2038, we will have a similar problem when a word of 32 bits will not be not enough to measure the seconds passed since 1970, a date format used by many Unix-based systems. Will we be ready? It would be necessary to recommend to future computer scientists more caution than the one applied by the space shuttle STS that did not fly the first days of the year in its lifetime, from 1981 to 2011, because it simply could not handle the change of year well.

I'M NOT A ROBOT

In 1950 the famous British mathematician Alan Turing (see we owe you an apology, 79) proposed an imitation game that would help discern whether a machine was intelligent or not. This game would play a pivotal role in artificial intelligence in the future, particularly in how we surf the Internet daily.

The game consists of having a judge and two subjects; one would be a human and the other a computer. The judge could not know the nature of the subjects, and for a computer to pass the test, for example, playing chess, it would have to pass it in a way that was indistinguishable from the human one.

Moving forward about fifty years, around 2000, we will find that many companies are having severe problems with machines posing as humans. For example, SPAM programs abused link insertion forms in search engines.

> *Computers are useless. They can only give us answers.*
>
> *— Attributed to Pablo Picasso, Spanish painter*

To the rescue comes a form of Turing test, sometimes called the reverse Turing test since a machine is the judge, and it comes as a curious acronym that we have all read while browsing: CAPTCHA.

CAPTCHA stands for Completely Automated Public Turing test to tell Computers and Humans Apart and is about presenting a tough test for a machine that a human can perform without too many complications.

So, when we find images deformed enough and with sufficiently complicated backgrounds that a machine cannot discern what it is, it is about protecting the site so that a computer cannot impersonate a human.

CAPTCHAs are not definitive. Multiple fronts are testing the concept: artificial intelligence, cheap labor used to pass the test, and even companies specialized in passing CAPTCHAs force research in this area to be in continuous movement.

SHAREWARE

In the times of the Internet, when we need new software, it is something as simple as opening our app store and downloading what we want. There may even be demo versions that we can try before we buy.

Was there anything like it before the Internet? The answer to this kind of question is almost always yes. It is usually accompanied by subtleties and solutions where the *social* word had a completely different meaning than it has today. This particular case follows that rule.

In the period when the CD-ROM had already been invented and the Internet was not yet widespread, a mode of software distribution flourished with a type of user agreement called shareware.

Shareware software was given free of charge to users, and users were not only allowed to share copies of the software but were encouraged to do so. The only con is that these used to be reduced versions, and the user was expected to buy the complete product by contacting the author if he liked the product.

An example would be the famous game Wolfenstein 3D from id Software, distributed as shareware with only the game's first episode.

Distribution was often done by the users themselves, in schools, cafeterias, and neighborhoods. But without a doubt, the moment of the greatest glory of shareware was when magazines began to include monthly a CD-ROM with thousands of shareware programs. More advanced users could obtain the latest shareware from their pre-internet networked systems such as BBS.

The advent of the Internet, FTP servers, and websites led to the demise of shareware as such, but its essence endures today on numerous platforms in the form of software that can be tested before buying.

Viruses, Worms, Trojans, and Other Bad Weeds

For many, the last of the great mathematicians is John Von Neumann, the great Hungarian genius (see the atypical genius, 82). He has among the many of his crea-tions no less than the Von Neu-mann architecture, on which all of our computers today run, and the quantum logic that defines how our future computers will work.

Well, with his theory of the self-reproducible automaton, this great genius also gave us the the-oretical basis of something more mundane but equally interesting, the theory that underpins com-puter viruses.

The first viruses were created and stayed within laboratories. Later, viruses began to jump into the world, from computer to computer, through floppy disks. Finally, the virus state-of-the-art evolved with viruses showing graphics such as the Ping-Pong virus or with sophis-ticated concealment systems.

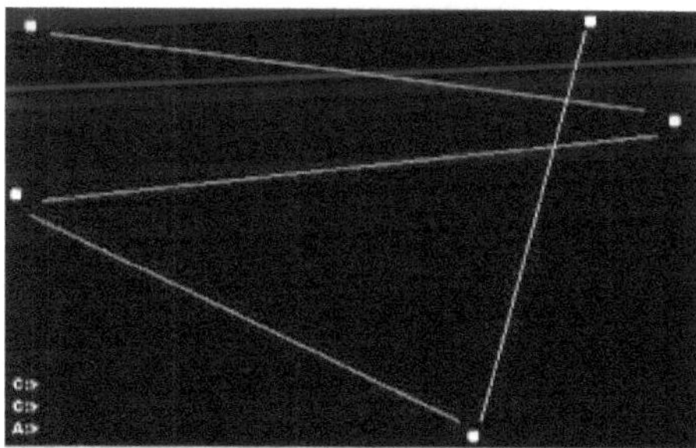

The Ping-Pong virus showed a ball bouncing off the edges of our screen if a disk was writ-ten precisely in the 30th minute of any hour.

The virus had no mali-cious intentions, but us-ing a code that only worked on computers with 8088 and 8086 CPUs caused it to create problems and data loss to users of 80286, 80386, 80486, etc.

All viruses are malware, but not all malware is viruses. In addition, it should be noted that there are different types of malware, such as:

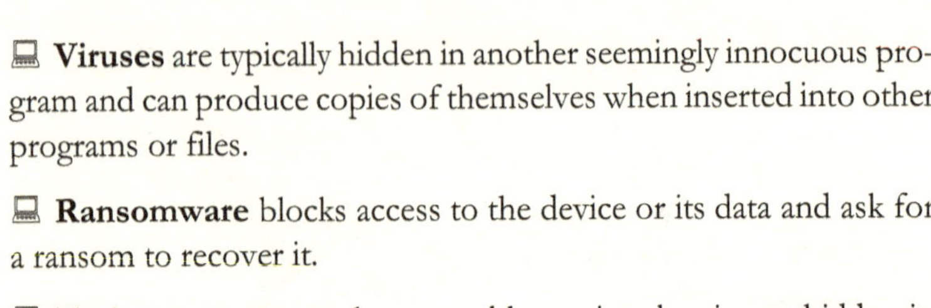 **Viruses** are typically hidden in another seemingly innocuous program and can produce copies of themselves when inserted into other programs or files.

Ransomware blocks access to the device or its data and ask for a ransom to recover it.

Trojans, a program that resembles a virus but is not hidden in another program, nor does it usually try to reproduce itself. Typically it is achieved by deceiving the user, for example, in an email.

Rootkits are programs that infect the operating system and modify it to become virtually invisible. They usually give a gateway to the attacker to do whatever they want with the device.

THE NAME UNIX

In the mid-'60s, MIT, Bell Labs, and General Electric were developing Multics, a new operating system that was very powerful but gigantic and full of complexities.

The development of Multics was going badly. The developers had lost all hope of finishing the project, even after leaving aside parts of the grandiloquent initial vision they had for it.

Frustrated by the impending failure, the engineers were abandoning one by one. Among the last to do so were Ken Thompson, who recently co-created the Go language, and Dennis Ritchie, creator of the C language, among many other achievements.

Instead of abandoning the idea altogether, these legendary programmers wanted to try again, focusing only on the best ideas and goals of Multics and discarding the rest. And that was how they managed to convince their superiors that a new operating system will be developed after several attempts.

> *UNIX is very simple, it just needs a genius to understand its simplicity.*
>
> *— Dennis Ritchie, co-creator of Unix and C*

This new operating system needed a name. And, like so many other ideas in computer science came as a joke. It would be called Unics

(Uniplexed Information and Computing Service) as a mockery of Multics (Multiplexed Information and Computer Services). It later went on to be written as Unix, a change that Brian Kernighan says no one remembers from where it came.

And so, it was with perseverance after a failure and with a joke, showing that humor is very present in computer science, that the all-time most influential operating system got its name.

ANCIENT GREECE AND THE DEMONS OF UNIX

Anyone who has used a variant of Unix, such as Linux, has been exposed to a type of program called a daemon.

They are programs that run as a resident process rather than being interactively executed by the user. A printing service or a service for the system log would be a good example. They are easily recognizable because their executables usually end with the letter d, e.g., `syslogd` or `sshd`.

In Greek mythology, the daemons were guiding spirits, transmitting the affairs of mortals to the gods and the divine to mortals. This analogy would be accurate enough if someone had already chosen the name daemon. However, the history behind this name is even more beautiful.

The use of daemon was not conceived by the creators of Unix but by the MIT laboratory called Project MAC. They called themselves a project with the sole intention of being able to borrow scientists from other laboratories with less bureaucracy, but they were a laboratory. The renowned computer scientist from Oakland, California, Fernando Corbató, pioneer of timeshare systems and Turing prize in 1990, decided to call demons after Maxwell's demon.

And what was Maxwell's demon? It is nothing more or less than a thought experiment created in 1867 by the Scottish physicist James Clerk Maxwell. In that experiment, Maxwell challenged the second law of thermodynamics (In an isolated system, entropy never decreases) with a tiny naughty demon that would play with the molecules of a container without interacting with them, using only information.

So, the Unix daemons were inspired by those of Project MAC, which in turn were inspired by a nineteenth-century physicist who drew on the demons of ancient Greece. To know the entire history, we only have to find out what inspired the ancient Greeks!

EASTER EGGS

In the 70s, the almighty Atari did not make concessions to its employees (see the dog who designed computers, 11). The games had no credits; only the company's name appeared in the box, no copyright was given, and there was no external recognition for the programmer or artists. According to some employees, they were even told that they were easily replaceable. For those reasons, many creators of Atari ended up leaving the company, some even created Activision, which today is still a giant in the world of video games, while Atari remains only a legend of the past.

Everything changed in 1979. In a David vs. Goliath fight, Warren Robinett faced the executives of New York to get recognition.

Warren was writing what would be the first action adventure, the adventure video game, where the player would have an adventure in which to look for a chalice that had been stolen and return it to where it always should have been the yellow castle. Along the way, the player had to find keys to open the other castles in addition to trying to avoid different dangers such as dragons or bats.

Warren created a whole genre, and it would have been a shame if no one remembered him for it. Inspired by the urban legends of his teenage years, it was said that the Beatles hid messages in their songs if they were played backward. Warren introduced on a game screen a very difficult-to-find message that said: Created by Warren Robinett.

Atari sold more than 200,000 copies of Adventure before anyone discovered Warren's secret message. Then, a 15-year-old boy from Salt Lake City, Utah, wrote a letter to Atari describing how to find the hidden message in detail.

Warren was not particularly concerned about the repercussions of the matter. He had no copyright that could take away from him, and by then, he had already left the company. But to his surprise, his small act of disobedience was welcomed at Atari.

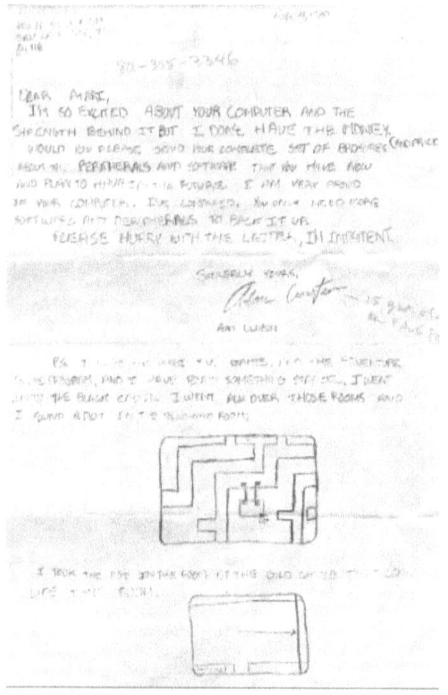

Although, at first, upon finding the message, Atari thought about retiring the game and rereleasing it, its new video game design leader Steven Wright thought it was pretty interesting to have surprises hidden in video games. It was like getting up on Easter morning, going outside, and finding Easter eggs hidden in the garden.

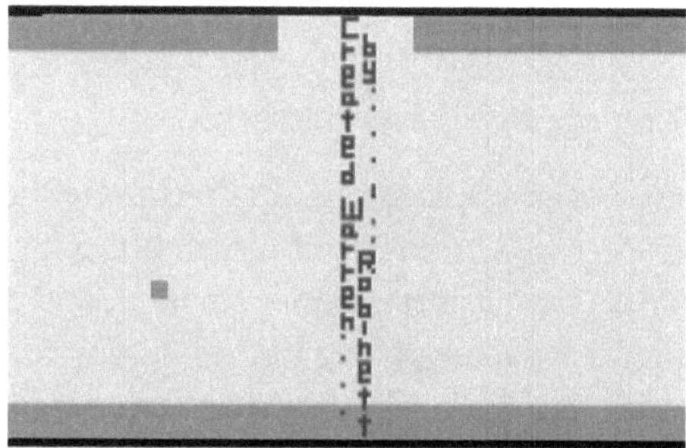

That's how Easter eggs were born in the software. Nowadays, it is a widespread practice, for example, Google Maps used to respond to requests for directions from New York to Tokyo by telling the user that he should cross the Pacific Ocean by kayak, but it is worth remembering that everything comes from the struggle of a little David, video game programmer, against a gigantic Goliath. And we already know who won.

KILLER APPS

How can a company sell a product that is not needed? While it is true that today it seems impossible to live without a cell phone or even a computer, there was a time when life was perfectly normal without them.

The first attempts to introduce computers to the general public creating a need, while imaginative, were not very successful. For example, in 1969, Neiman Marcus tried to sell the Honeywell Kitchen Computer, a computer designed specifically for the kitchen.

Using the computer required training of about two weeks, the data entry was done with toggle switches, and the output was given in binary coding lights. It also had an integrated cutting board and brought some built-in recipes. Unfortunately, the advertising, in line with its time, would not pass any of the modern standards regarding gender equality. There is no evidence that a single unit was ever purchased.

There were, however, applications that did know how to become indispensable. Perhaps the first and most important was imagined, in 1978, by a Harvard business school student named Dan Bricklin. Dan was sitting in a class watching his accounting teacher as he calculated and recalculated the cells drawn on the board. But, of course, that's precisely what accountants worldwide did; it was tedious and boring.

Dan had worked as a programmer before entering business school and didn't quite understand why they didn't do it on a computer instead of on a piece of paper. So Dan wrote an electronic spreadsheet for Apple II computers: VisiCalc. It was an immediate success.

Steve Jobs himself acknowledged that VisiCalc had propelled the Apple II to success. The usefulness and versatility of VisiCalc were such that consumers bought Apple II computers to be able to use VisiCalc, and that's how the first Killer App was born.

The marketing experts of each new platform released: video game consoles, phones, tablets, virtual reality, quantum computing, etc., first ask themselves what will be the killer app to make the platform successful.

Some killer apps

Lotus 1-2-3. InfoWorld magazine went so far as to say: let's call it by its name, let's not say compatible PC but compatible Lotus 1-2-3.

PowerPoint, the reputed presentation system acquired by MicroSoft. The Wall Street Journal quoted a professional: people will buy a Macintosh to access PowerPoint.

Super Mario Bros, has been a killer app for all Nintendo consoles.

Half-Life: Alyx, sales of the Valve Index virtual reality system rose dramatically by announcing a sequel to Half-Life that almost counts as a third part (see valve and third parts, 44).

CRYPTOCURRENCIES

In 2008, amid what we now call the Great Recession, confidence in banks and the ability of governments to control the economy were more in question than ever.

In that same year, somewhere in the world, a mysterious person whom we only know his alias: Satoshi Nakamoto, wrote an article explaining how a virtual currency would work that would not need a central bank but would use a system of mutual trust. Its creation was called Bitcoin.

He recorded his intentions in a somewhat mysterious way. For example, in the first bitcoin transaction, he included the cover title of the times magazine of January 3, 2009, which referred to a possible second bank bailout.

That was the rebellious spirit of Bitcoin. There were no banks, and there was no government control. It was just a series of bits that identify a currency, and many computers on the Internet, the so-called miners responsible for validating transactions. In addition, they also minted new coins through a complicated mathematical process, which despite being expensive to calculate, in the end, returned value in the form of a Bitcoin.

Bitcoin also had a particularity; it was open source (see free software, 20). This created the possibility of creating other cryptocurrencies with relative simplicity. The following stories are legend: transaction websites hacked and hundreds of millions were lost, and pizzas for which 10,000 Bitcoins were paid (with a dollar value that some years later reached over 100 million).

Even today, we are still writing about whether Bitcoin or any other cryptocurrency can one day be able to carry out the same transactions per second as any credit card network, something that is still a long way off, and whether its value is due more to a bubble (in 2018 it came down from about $ 20,000 to just over $ 3,000) than the intrinsic value it may have.

It isn't easy to know for sure the answer to these unknowns or what the future of cryptocurrencies will be, but what we can know for sure is that the technology underneath, the so-called blockchain, is being used for numerous and exciting applications such as to improve the traceability of the use of money donated to non-profit organizations. Hence, donors are calmer seeing how exactly their donation is used. Therefore, whoever you are, wherever you are, thank you, Satoshi.

Software

DEEPFAKES

If we stopped to look back every five years and see how much technology has changed the world, we would be amazed. Yet, every day we take for granted very sophisticated technologies that were just a few years ago simply science fiction.

Technologies often bring overwhelmingly positive changes. Fields such as medicine attest to these benefits. However, when we talk about something like software, which has almost unlimited possibilities, it is natural that advances that can be labeled as questionable if viewed from a certain perspective will appear.

An example would be deepfakes, a word game uniting deep learning and fake. It is typically used to create fake videos (or images). They would replace someone's face, or even what someone seems to be saying, with the face of whoever we wanted or whatever we wanted them to say.

The art of image modification is ancient, predating even the digital age. The modifications of the photos ordered by Stalin to remove his disgraced comrades are well known. The big difference between the ultra-fake with their predecessors is that they come very close to perfection.

Recently deepfakes have been used to pretend that politicians were drunk or that they gave messages that they never gave in reality. The adverse effects these videos can have are gigantic. Remember, the quality is so high that the videos are almost indistinguishable from a true ones. They have also been used to put the face of celebrities in videos of a pornographic nature or even simply as a mockery.

With all these harmful applications, one would think, shouldn't deepfakes be banned? Maybe so, but what would we think when we know that the same technology is used to finish films on whose actors, unfortunately, we cannot count on anymore, as happened in Rogue One with the beloved Carrie Fisher, or for the age progression of portraits, such as those used by the police in cases of missing persons and even to improve the definition of old movies or video games.

> *Anyone with a computer and internet access can produce an ultra-fake video.*
>
> *— John Villasenor, professor in UCLA*

All these applications are based almost entirely on the same principle on which deepfakes are based, the antagonistic generative networks. So if some applications were banned, it would probably end up banning the others. Luckily there are already ongoing investigations of other neural networks that will try to detect the deepfakes that our eye cannot detect. Although this undoubtedly creates a mouse and cat type situation, as it happens with captchas (see I'm not a robot, 23), it can alleviate to some extent the negative consequences that deepfakes have on our society without excessively affecting the benefits.

PORTABLE MUSIC

In the '70s, the devices for listening to music were becoming proudly large. On the street, the best radio cassette was the largest and most powerful. Styles of music, urban tribes, and even dances grew and lived under these premises.

At that time, Masaru Ibuka, co-founder of Sony, always traveled with an audio recorder with tapes to enjoy his great hobby, the opera. But, unfortunately, that kind of recorder was designed more for a journalist or a secretary than a music fan, giving him a great idea. He asked his engineering chief to remove everything superfluous from the recorder, such as the ability to record itself and create the smallest possible player.

That's how, in 1979, by introducing the Walkman, Sony changed music forever. With it, Sony influenced music and culture internationally as never before and set the bar very high. Then, of course, there were some improvements in the following decades, such as the Minidisc or the Discman, but you could not talk about a substantial improvement in the market until much later.

> *As long as there are batteries in my Walkman, I'm fine.*
>
> *— Eminem, American rapper*

But was there any improvement that didn't reach the markets? Yes, there was, and it was created precisely in the same year, 1979. Two Englishmen, Kane Kramer and James Campbell, aged 23 and 21, had the vision of a portable player with solid-state memory: the IXI System. At that time, the memory they proposed could barely store only one song,

assuming it was not very long. Kane and James thought this was not a problem because they expected significant memory technology improvements in a short time. Unfortunately, they were wrong; they even ended up losing the use of their patents by not using them enough.

Hoping for better hardware to be developed was one way to fix the problem. But history and the excellent German engineering of Karlheinz Brandenburg have taught us that there was another way.

While studying at the University of Erlangen-Nuremberg, Karlheinz received a request from his professor to find a way to send music over an ISDN line. The trick was to compress it without detriment to the listening experience.

Suzanne Vega's Tom's Diner was playing on one of his walks through the college corridors. Karlheinz felt electrified, as he mentioned in an interview years later: *I was ready to make the final adjustments to the algorithm... somewhere in the corridor, Tom's Diner was playing on a radio. I felt electrified.* He knew it would be almost impossible to compress this warm a cappella voice. That's how, somehow, Tom's Diner had become his Lena (see image processing and playboy, 93).

Karlheinz ended up creating the MP3 compressed audio format with his algorithm. It compressed the music so much that a CD could fit up to 150 songs, although this depended on various factors such as the length of the song or the quality sought.

MP3 revolutionized music like it hadn't been done since the days of the Walkman and opened the door to other technologies like P2P (see peer-to-peer networks, 68). Incidentally, it also taught us that sometimes, as the creators of the IXI System learned, there is no need to entrust everything to the hardware; software often has an ace up its sleeve.

Years later, Apple created the successful iPod based on the inventions of Kane Kramer, the IXI, and Karlheinz, the MP3. Unfortunately, as we know, Kane lost his patent, so Apple didn't even bother to recognize him as the father of the iPod. But in a twist of fate, amid a legal battle over patents allegedly used on the iPod between Apple and Burst.com, Apple found it convenient to recognize Kane as the father of the iPod since he had no patent; therefore, it would cost them nothing and would protect them from accusations of Burst.com.

Kane went to California and helped Apple in its litigation. He stated that he was only paid for the trip's expenses and was given an iPod for free, although it broke a few months later. It will always remain a historical fact that, at least, he was publicly recognized as the father of the iPod.

THE SOFTWARE CAN BE DEADLY

In the '80s, the Canadian company AECL developed the third version of its radiation therapy machine, the Therac-25. It was the replacement for the Therac-6 and Therac-20.

Unlike its predecessors, the Therac-25 was not manually operated. Instead, everything was controlled by software. To make the software control possible, all the manual control systems in the previous versions were removed, and some of the hardware security systems also had to be removed.

In 1983 the machine went into service and helped thousands of patients without incident until June 3, 1985, the 61-year-old patient Katie Yarborough, a beauty salon manicurist, was being treated for breast cancer. During the treatment, she felt terrible pain. Immediately afterward, she complained about what had happened. So, the oncologist and Tim Still, the center's physiologist, examined both her and the machine but didn't see anything out of the ordinary. Even so, Tim exquisitely fulfilled his obligation and contacted the manufacturer to ask if there might have been an overdose, but he was ignored.

Two weeks later, Katie returned complaining of tingling and worsening pains. He also had a pinkish circle on his back that excessive radiation could explain. Tim spent that night trying to reproduce the intensity that would have been needed for such excess radiation, but he failed; every time he set parameters that could reproduce such radiation, the software safety systems of the machine stopped the treatment. Nevertheless, Tim continued to insist on the company and discuss the problem with other professionals and associations. He even received a threatening call from AECL to give up. Eventually, Katie lost the mobility of her left arm.

Just seven weeks after Katie's incident, another woman was overexposed to radiation by the machine. The autopsy revealed that she died from cancer she was being treated for, but if she had survived, Katie would have needed a hip change due to her overexposure. Later a Man from Texas was being treated, and the pain was such that the treatment ended with his knocks on the door while trying to flee the room. Regrettably, he died a few weeks later from the effects of radiation. Other fatal incidents regrettably happened in 1986 and 1987.

Among the causes of all these exposures was a software error in how keyboard input was processed, although other bugs, documentation problems, and useless error messages mixed with important error messages were also discovered.

> *When a program grows in potential by an evolution of patches and fixes not fully understood, the programmer begins to lose track of the internal details, loses his ability to predict what will happen, instead begins to assume with hope instead of knowing, and begins to see the result as if the program were an unpredictable individual.*
>
> *— Marvin Minsky, one of the fathers of artificial intelligence*

Computer science can be enjoyable, but it's certainly not a game. Also, while it can be very lucrative for a company, it can't just be measured in business revenue. Quality control and the engineering process are not optional, even when you are programming a utility unrelated to medicine, the military, etc. For example, even if a Microsoft programmer didn't think he was doing something critical when programming Windows, there was a time when aircraft carriers and tanks worked with Windows.

One would think that the deaths caused by the Therac-25 were not in vain and that this lesson was learned. But unfortunately, these kinds of incidents never wholly disappeared. We have a relatively recent example: in 2018, 189 people died aboard a Boeing 737 MAX from software issues. Later, in 2019, 157 perished in the same aircraft model from the same software issues.

Games

Play is the highest form of research

— Albert Einstein, German physicist

THE FIRST VIDEOGAME

William Higinbotham was involved in developing the atomic bomb and developing the radar monitor of the experimental B-28 bomber. In addition, he was a notable activist for the non-proliferation of nuclear weapons, a fact he preferred to be remembered.

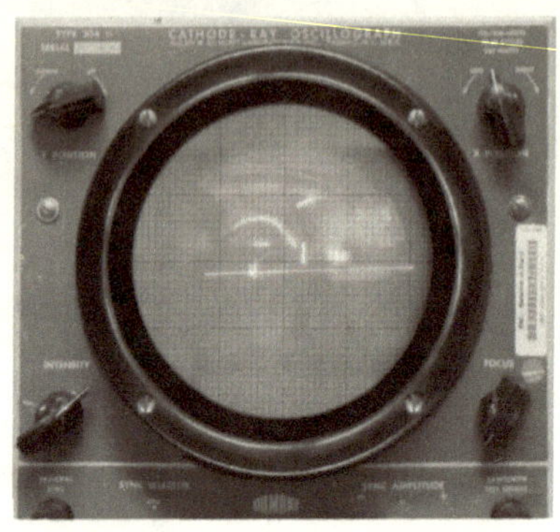

One day, while thinking about something dynamic and engaging to prepare for a science fair, he made use of a tube-based computer and an oscilloscope to create a small tennis simulation game called Tennis for Two. The game was a hit at the show, but William never considered patenting it.

This fact was almost forgotten, and it was not until the '80s that some modern archaeology was done to bring it to light. Interestingly, although William and his team assembled Tennis for Two in two weeks, the team that tried to rebuild it in 1997 for the 50th anniversary of its creation took more than three months.

Was this the first video game? It's hard to say, not because there's anything before Tennis for Two, but because it's hard to decide if this was a video game. The consensus is that it seems that it was not, given that there was no video monitor but an oscilloscope, and of course, they are called video games, not oscilloscope games.

The honor of being the first video game would fall on Spacewar!, created in 1961 by Stephen Russell, or at least this is it for many. Although what is the first video game is a fact still debated, some contenders would be: OXO, Alan Turing's Turochamp (see we owe you an apology, 79), and Cathode-Ray Amusement Device.

Spacewar! was a small spaceship

combat game created to demonstrate the possibilities of a PDP-1 computer and ended up serving as the foundation for the creation of the entire video game industry.

> ### Don't miss it
>
> Stephen Russell is a volunteer at the very entertaining California Museum of Computer History. He kindly shows Space Wars! in a PDP-1 restored by the museum. So if you visit the museum of the history of computing, do not miss it!

A GUY CALLED BRUSH

In the late '70s, there was a type of game called *conversational adventure*. They were games typically centered around a text that described a character's situation at one point in their adventure. The player had to write down the action he wanted the player to do, e.g., *take a hammer*, or *hit a lock*.

With the arrival of more powerful computers, it was possible to introduce graphics, and the so-called graphic adventure appeared, one of the genres that provokes the most sighs to veteran players. These games showed a scene in which you often had to use the

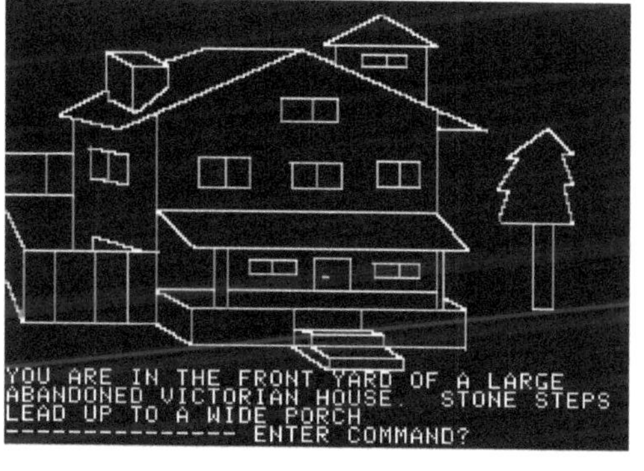

mouse to perform actions that solved the problems that arose, called in the world of video game design *puzzles,* to advance in the adventure.

By the early 90s, the graphic adventure had reached its zenith. Venerable games that are legend today were published: *The secret of Monkey Island, Indiana Jones and the fate of Atlantis, King Quest, Leisure Suit Larry,* etc.

Undoubtedly, The Secret of Monkey Island was the most famous graphic adventure of the '90s. Of it, its beloved main protagonist,

Guybrush Threepwood, remains one of the most recognizable icons in video games.

Interestingly, the name Guybrush was given by a killer app of the famous Commodore Amiga computer (see killer apps, 30) called *Deluxe Paint.* It was an image drawing application made in-house by Electronic Arts for its video game production. Still, it reached such a quality that it was published for external use. It was on the Amiga platform where it became predominant by being included in all units by an agreement between EA and Commodore that lasted until the bankruptcy of Commodore in 1994.

Amiga had support for long-length extensions, so the Amiga Deluxe Paint saved the brushes, images designed to be superimposed on other images, with the extension `.brush`.

> *My name is Guybrush Threepwood,*
> *and I want to be a pirate!*
>
> *- Guybrush Threepwood, character from Monkey Island*

At that time in LucasArts, the creators of Monkey Island were not very clear about what they wanted to call their main character, so they baptized him generically with *guy,* and as in the PC platform in which they worked, there could be no extensions of more than three characters (the extension of a brush on PC was `.bbm`) and probably because of the custom of using Commodore Amiga, brush was written in the name of the file leaving finally `guybrush.bbm`. The rest of the team thought that was his real name, and it happened that Guybrush was left as the final name. The surname came from an internal competition in the company looking for a funny surname.

ALL YOUR BASE ARE BELONG TO US

In the internet age, memes are born and die in the blink of an eye. A successful meme will typically last between four and six months. Few memes reach Olympus exceeding that figure, which does not necessarily make them permanent, only somewhat long-lived.

However, there is a legendary meme from before the advent of Reddit, Youtube, Facebook, and Tumblr, which has crossed continents, platforms, and services; it has been repeated on television, radio, and even by a congresswoman from the United States of America. We are talking about the venerable: *All your base are belong to us.*

It started in 1989 when the Japanese company Toaplan released its arcade video game Zero Wing. But, like so many other arcade shoot 'em ups of the time, the game had no plot. Instead, it was just about destroying enemy ships.

It was decided that the game needed a story to take it home, so when the game was ported to the Megadrive console, particularly for the European edition, some cinematic scenes were added with a 

terrible translation from Japanese to English, in a phenomenon that is known as the *Engrlish*, ironic variant of the word *English* as if a Japanese person mispronounced it. It is used to indicate erroneous English, resulting from a translation terrible enough to be considered funny.

The scene where *All your base are belong to us* is mentioned, became an animation and was distributed in the popular Forums Something Awful. From there, it jumped from platform to platform until it became the myth we know today.

Therefore, the meme was born in a Japanese arcade, but took shape in a Sega Megadrive in Europe, then reached forums in the United States, where it survived all the changes in online platforms to reach us more than two decades later.

Some uses of All your base are belong to us

💻 2003 **Wired magazine** reports on the phenomenon

💻 2004 game **Rome: Total War** shows the phrase said by the enemy AI while conducting diplomacy

💻 2006 **Youtube** interrupted its service for maintenance, the phrase appeared under the Youtube logo, and many believed it was a hack.

💻 2013 In the Android game store **Google Play Games**, if the Konami code (see Konami code, 47) was made on the touch screen, it was discovered as an easter egg (see easter eggs, 28).

💻 2019 The well-known congresswoman **Alexandria Ocasio-Cortez** twitted *All your base (are) belong to us.*

VALVE AND THIRD PARTS

In 1983 Gabe Newell, a Harvard student, left his studies at the prestigious university to work in a young company called Microsoft. Gabe worked there for thirteen years on projects such as Windows and OS/2. Even though dropping off Harvard doesn't sound like a great idea, Gabe made the right bet. Microsoft made him rich.

A colleague of Gabe's, Michael Abrash, left Microsoft to work at id Software on the legendary game Quake. This inspired Gabe so much that, alongside another colleague, Mike Harrington, he decided to use his good financial situation to found a video game company. The problem at the time was that they had no experience developing video games, so it was precisely Michael Abrash who introduced him to video game legend and id Software founder John Carmack. He convinced them to license the Quake engine to make their games, and that's what they did.

Gabe and Mike created Valve, and Valve's first creation was one of the most revered games in video game history: Half-Life. Later came resounding successes such as Team Fortress Classic, Counter-Strike, Counter-Strike GO, Half-Life 2, Team Fortress 2, Portal, Portal 2, Left 4 Dead, Left 4 Dead 2, Dota, and Dota2. However, an evident pattern can be seen here. Valve has never created a third part despite announcing such revered games as Half-life as a trilogy.

> *So, maybe someday, the number two will lead us to that shiny integer glowing on the mountain someplace.*
>
> — *Gabe Newell, founder of Valve*

For the first few years after Half-Life 2, Gabe talked about completing the trilogy, but his statements faded over time until they reached a re-sounding: *we have nothing to say about Half-Life 3*. The gamer community, desperate for the desire to play the sequel, started an epic meme about Valve's inability to count to three, from parents recording their children's tear-jerking reactions by letting them play Half-Life and Half-Life 2 and telling them that Half-Life 3 was never made, to Gabe himself, embracing the meme saying in his voicemails for Dota: *you have killed more than two people but less than four.*

In November 2019, the release of Half-Life 3 was expected. The community was excited about the possibility, and good old Gabe's, perhaps joking again, introduced them to Half-Life Alyx, a virtual reality game in the Half-Life universe. The expectation was such that in just 24 hours, the video of the presentation reached ten million views.

It's not Half-Life 3, but at least it's something the community can entertain themselves with while still dreaming.

MARIO BROS AND SPINACH

At the beginning of the '80s Nintendo, which at that time made arcade machines, wanted to assault the American market. However, they had already tried without success. The game Radar Scope, for example, ended up with numerous machines in stock unsold.

Nintendo's president decided it was a good idea to reuse the unsold machines to make some other game since his best employees were busy with more important projects. So he asked a then-unknown Shigeru Miyamoto if he could take care of the project. Shigeru bravely accepted what would be his first design project. This decision was fortunate for the rest of the video game fans since later, and thanks to this experience, Shigeru would become the most famous video game designer in history. To him, we owe masterpieces like The Legend of Zelda.

To make sure that the American public saw this new game closely, the president of Nintendo tried to get a license to use the characters of Popeye the sailor in the game. They started designing the game with Popeye in mind but soon concluded that getting the rights would not be possible. So, Shigeru redesigned the game around three other characters: a carpenter, a gorilla, and the bride; a love triangle similar to Popeye, Brutus, and Olivia but distinct enough not to need a license. The game was called Donkey Kong.

When the game was delivered to Nintendo America, it was received with misgivings. It was too different from what they were used. So they Americanized it a bit by calling the bride Pauline, after Polly James, the wife of the warehouse manager. In addition, the carpenter was given Jumpman for being a name similar to well-known brands such as Walkman (see portable music, 34) and Pac-Man. However, it was later changed to Mario for the resemblance to Mario Segale, the landlord of the Nintendo office of America.

Eventually, two bar owners in Seattle, Washington, were convinced to place the machine. At first, they were very reluctant, but when they saw the revenue, they asked for more units, thus opening the way to the serial production of the video game that gave birth to the most famous video game character of all time: Super Mario.

What would have become of the history of video games if Nintendo had obtained that license from Popeye the sailor?

KONAMI CODE

In the mid-'80s, the young Japanese programmer Kazuhisa Hashimoto, while working for Konami, was creating the Nintendo Entertainment System (NES) version of the popular arcade game *Gradius* but encountered an unexpected problem: he was not able to pass the game. Therefore he could not verify that he had not introduced bugs (see a very real bug, 7).

Then Kazuhisa made a simple but historic decision, introducing a code, that is, a sequence of joystick movements and button presses, which, if executed correctly, gave the player all the improvements available in the game. The sequence was: ↑ ↑ ↓ ↓ ← → ← → B A (Start).

It certainly helped him to finish the game quickly and to be able to try it as he wanted. However, there was a slight problem; he forgot to remove the code before the game's final version was made, and it was pre-

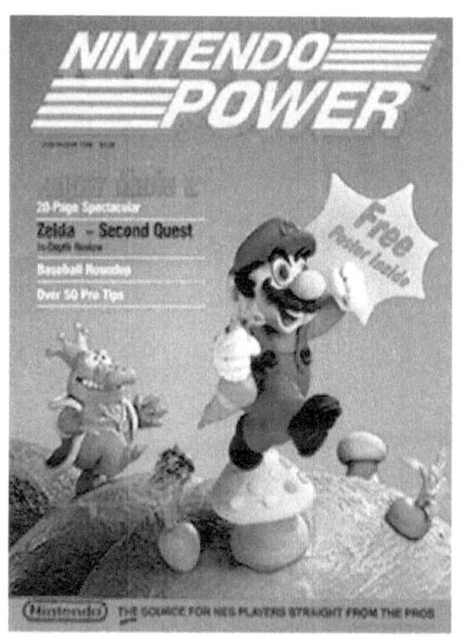

cisely at that moment that the first video game *trick* was created, until today is known as *the Konami code.*

At Konami they realized what happened a little later but decided to leave the code there because it was simple enough to be remembered but complex enough for someone to execute it by accident. So not only was it used in Gradius, but it was also added to other Konami games.

Although the code was known to the developers, the general public did not know about it until the NES version of Contra was created (in fact, the code is sometimes called the Contra code). Then, Nintendo published in Nintendo Power magazine the hitherto secret code.

The code was used not only in Konami games but also by many other developers. Although somehow it was born by mistake, it became a legend among video game players who still avidly test the code in each game they find today to see if they are lucky.

Some uses of Konami Code

⌨ 2009 On **Facebook** activates an Easter egg (see easter eggs, 28), activating a lens glow effect.

⌨ 2012 In the Disney film **Break Ralph!** in a fundamental part of history.

⌨ 2012 Appears as a question in the American version of **Who wants to be a millionaire?** The contestant decided not to answer and lost $7,000.

⌨ 2013 In the series **Family Guy**, its protagonist proposes it in the Space Cadet chapter.

⌨ 2017 **The Bank of Canada** activates an Easter egg with fireworks and the reproduction of the song O Canada on its website.

ANTI-COPYING SYSTEMS

Software piracy is almost as old as proprietary software. Proof of this is perhaps a famous missive that the young Bill Gates launched in 1976 from what was then a tiny startup called Microsoft.

In it, he asked hobbyists not to copy the perforated paper tapes of his Altair Basic (you read that correctly, perforated paper tapes, as this predates even magnetic tape or floppy disk) because it was unfair to software developers.

Later, with the advent of floppy disks, some developers stopped making calls to morality and took action. When manufacturing floppy disks, they introduced minor errors that did not interfere with the operation of their software but prevented the duplication of software from working. The first PC game on sale, Microsoft Adventure, had this kind of protection.

It meant that something as fragile as a floppy disk could not be backed up and did not allow programs to be installed on the hard drive. It didn't take long for protection to be bypassed by crackers (hackers specializing in jumping anti-copy systems), so pirated copies were often more comfortable to use and maintain than the originals.

Both publishers and users hated this type of copy protection, so especially in the world of games, a whole new type of protection called the off-disk copy protection arose. This protection usually required giving the game when starting a word or some kind of data present in the instruction manual on a page and paragraph specified by the game.

Pirates tried to keep copying games by simply copying the manuals, but these became increasingly sophisticated. They became, for example, manuals printed in inks that could only be seen through a small filter (so that it could not be easily photocopied) or wheels with small perforations that could only be easily copied if partially destroyed, as was the case with Monkey Island (see a guy called brush, 41). Another interesting example was Alone in the dark, which provided a little booklet just a little bigger than a thumb, with many pages, so copying it was arduous.

After some short flirtations with uncomfortable systems such as dongles, small non-copyable hardware devices that had to be connected to the computer, or continuous validation with the need to be online, the industry ended up giving an almost deadly blow to piracy with the creation of online platforms such as Steam, from Valve (see valve and third parts, 44) that make it so easy to buy and use video games that most of the public decides not even to consider piracy.

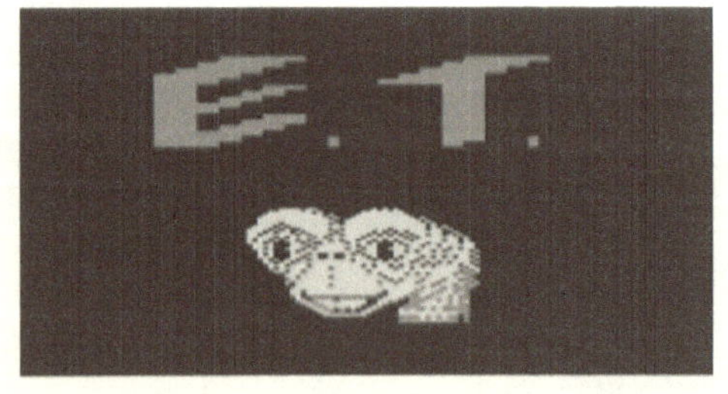

And for the few that do, games sometimes have small mechanisms to make the game less entertaining for the pirate or even give moralizing messages, as in the case of Bezerk Studios' *Just Shapes and Beats*. So, this is interestingly the point where we started with Bill Gates' missive, has the industry come full circle?

THE LEGEND OF ATARI'S E.T.

By 1983 the video game industry had become a tremendously difficult arena to compete. The market was saturated with low-quality clone games, and manufacturers were creating consoles that were incompatible even with their other consoles.

This situation caused consumer confidence in video games to falter. Is this console the one that the manufacturer will continue to support? Is this game a good game or another of those many clone fiascos?

Some manufacturers chose to make games about franchises to try to ensure success. For example, Atari created a game about the movie *In Search of the Lost Ark* with some success, and Steven Spielberg was delighted.

When E.T, the next film, arrived, it was logical that Spielberg would go back to Atari and ask that the work be done by the same programmer: Howard Scott Warshaw, who, by the way, is a pioneer of Easter eggs (see easter eggs, 28).

What could go wrong? Same company, same programmer. Only one thing changed, *in search of the lost ark* was developed in seven months, and E.T. had to be completed before the Christmas campaign, that is, in six weeks. Warshaw did his best in those weeks, but the result was considered by many the worst game in the history of video games.

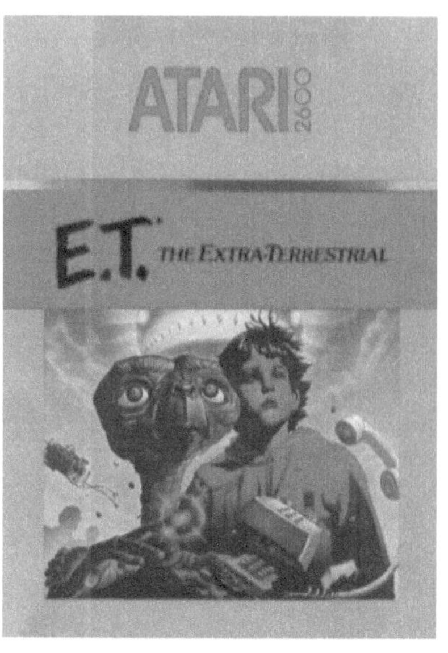

Atari, confident by the success of *In Search of the Lost Ark*, decided to skip the audience tests and began manufacturing five million copies of the game, of which only 1.5 million were sold. Of these, many were returned when consumers tried the game. Finally, according to Atari Next Gen magazine, Atari raised 25 million but invested 100 million with E.T. This event is considered one of the fundamental factors of the video game crisis of 1983, which ended up practically making Atari disappear forever.

> *Atari is a very sad story.*
>
> —*Steve Wozniak, Co-Founder of Apple Inc.*

The debacle of the game and the passage of time created a legend that lasted almost three decades. Atari, which did not know what to do with the game it had already tried to sell in every possible way, even devalued from $49.95 to $1, was thought to have buried all the leftover copies in the desert, as reported in 1983 by the Alamogordo Daily News of New Mexico.

It was not entirely proven and ended up recorded as a meme in the popular imagination. Even the musical band Wintergreen used the legend in the music video for their song *When I wake up*. It was not uncommon for amateurs to travel to the desert shovel in hand, to try to discover the already mythological site.

Three decades later, the legend would cease to be a legend. Microsoft embarked on creating a documentary for Xbox, decided to cover Atari's story, and end doubts about E.T. by sending a professional excavation team into the desert.

There, beginning on April 26, 2014, along with the Microsoft team, Warshaw and Ernest Cline, author of Ready Player One and video game fans who had made a pilgrimage to the desert, were able to witness the first find of archaeological video game excavation of all time, where the authentic resting place of E.T. cartridges and other games was found.

Only 1,178 of the estimated 700,000 were extracted because the remains were deeper than expected, and their extraction would have been challenging. Only 10% of the games extracted were copies of E.T., so somehow the legend can continue. What is waiting down in the deepest parts?

THE BEST GAME THAT NEVER EXISTED

It was the early '80s, the golden age of arcades. At that time, the euphoria for them was such that they constantly appeared on television, and even large productions focused on games were filmed.

On a good day in 1981, to some rooms located just outside Portland, Oregon, filled at that moment with legendarily successful arcades such as Space invaders, Pac-Man, Missile Command, or Donkey Kong, a new machine arrived that inevitably attracted the attention of all players: *Polybius*.

The appearance of the cabinet could be described as rather weird, and the game was even stranger. It was a fast game riddled with abstract forms. Everyone who tried it claimed that it was highly addictive. The machine was copyrighted in 1981 and was signed by a company called with a German name: *Sinnesloschen Inc.*

The success of the machine in the halls was unstoppable, lines formed to be able to play, and there were even minor altercations caused by who would be the next player. In addition to a terrible addiction to it, those who played suffered effects such as amnesia, insomnia, nightmares, and hallucinations.

The machine disappeared from the arcades just a month after it arrived. The strangest thing is that while they were in the halls, the machines were periodically visited by *men in black* who connected to them to extract information.

For years it was discussed what the origin of this machine could be. The alleged German company *Sinnesloschen Inc.* was clearly a cover. The name wasn't entirely correct in German and would mean something akin to *sensory deprivation*. One of the most supported possibilities is that it was a CIA mind control experiment.

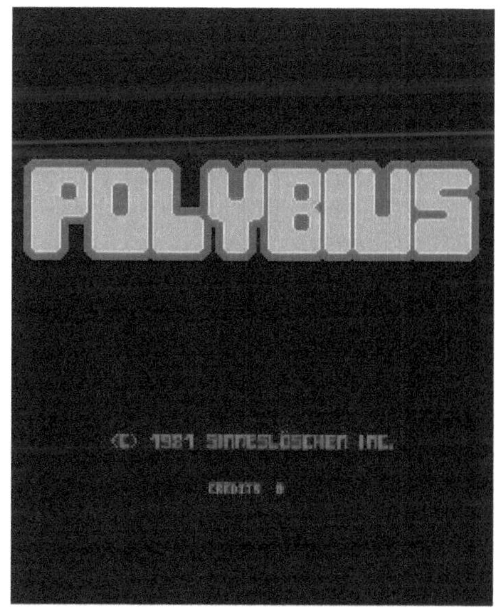

The story seems like a lie, and in fact, it is. Polybius is an urban legend with years of antiquity. It has been fed in forums without any tangible evidence to support it, not even copyright records.

The hysteria reached the point that a request was made to the FBI through an E-FOIA (Freedom of Information Act, abbreviated FOIA) asking it to release any information it had. Needless to say, the FBI found nothing about it.

It is suspected that the origin may be in Usenet, an old forum system (see Email predates the Internet, 56), possibly distorting over time what happened with the game Tempest, with which there were cases of epileptic seizures.

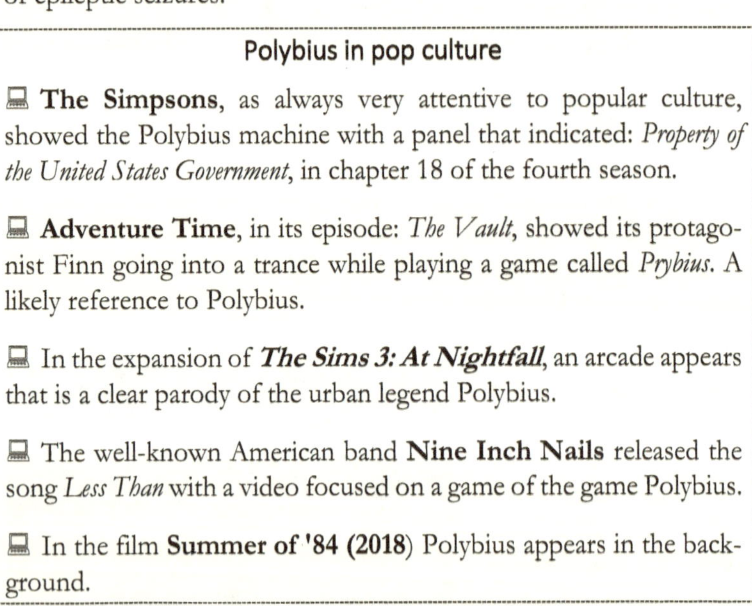

Polybius in pop culture

⌨ **The Simpsons**, as always very attentive to popular culture, showed the Polybius machine with a panel that indicated: *Property of the United States Government*, in chapter 18 of the fourth season.

⌨ **Adventure Time**, in its episode: *The Vault*, showed its protagonist Finn going into a trance while playing a game called *Prybius*. A likely reference to Polybius.

⌨ In the expansion of ***The Sims 3: At Nightfall***, an arcade appears that is a clear parody of the urban legend Polybius.

⌨ The well-known American band **Nine Inch Nails** released the song *Less Than* with a video focused on a game of the game Polybius.

⌨ In the film **Summer of '84 (2018)** Polybius appears in the background.

Internet

> *Getting information off the internet is like taking a drink from a fire hydrant.*
>
> — *Mitchell Kapor, Designer of Lotus 1-2-3*

EMAIL PREDATES THE INTERNET

For those who lived through the birth of the Internet, it is difficult to separate the @ symbol from the idea of the Internet. At that time, the word email was almost synonymous with the Internet. That symbol, so typical of email addresses, was the one that had made us use that keyboard key that nobody had ever given importance to before. The symbol also quickly became the new obsession in the industry of marketing.

However, two ideas we have, as intertwined as the Internet and email, do not even have the same antiquity. Email predates the Internet by a wide margin.

It all started in the sixties, with timeshare machines and large computers to which users connected with *dumb terminals*. In MIT's timeshare system, a program called MAIL was created that saved messages in a file called MAILBOX that the receiving user could only read. As you might expect, this command only served to send messages to users of the same computer.

Over the years, different utilities such as the possibility of attaching files and having aliases and distribution lists were included in this and other local messaging programs. As a result, it was already beginning to resemble the email we know today, but remember that it still stuck to a single computer to which many users can connect.

When ARPANET, a network of computers created by the United States Department of Defense that we could consider the mother of the Internet, was created, a wide network of computers with a well-defined communication system was finally created so that the doors were opened to innovations such as network email.

Ray Tomlinson created in 1971 the email system we know today. Since then, you could send mail between different machines, but how to separate the user's name from the server that would receive the mail at the address? Ray came up with the best solution. He would use the @ symbol that in English reads *at* so the address `user@server.local` would read: *user at server.local.*

> *What are the benefits of talking to your followers via email?*
> *It's quicker, easier, and involves less licking.*
>
> — *Douglas Adams, writer of The Hitchhiker's Guide to the Galaxy*

At that time, the Internet did not yet exist, and other networks like CSNET, JANET, BITNET, X.400, and FidoNet were seriously competing with ARPANET. Each with different forms of communication, such as direct phone calls between computers using modems to exchange the emails of different users.

The concept of being able to send emails between different organizations was one of the forces that led to the advent of the Internet itself. But, unfortunately, along with the Internet and simple and universal email came something not so desirable, SPAM!

THE GUARDIANS OF THE SEVEN KEYS

One of the significant differences between what was Arpanet, the network created with military funds that gave rise to the Internet, and the Internet itself is how the connected servers are named.

When a device connects to the Internet directly, it is assigned an IPv4 address, although it could also be IPv6, in which case everything below applies similarly. An IPv4 address is four numbers ranging from 0 to 255 and separated by periods. This number identifies the device in the great world wide web that is the Internet in a similar way to how a car's license plate uniquely identifies our car.

As you would expect, the need to give names to IP addresses to make them more memorable was recognized from very early on. It is more comfortable for a user to remember and type the name of their preferred search engine than to remember four numbers.

To do this, a file called `hosts` was created, and all the known names were in it. In principle, when there were only a handful of machines in Arpanet, they synchronized between machines. However, after that resulted in chaos, it ended up being centralized at the Stanford

Research Institute (SRI), where Douglas Engelbart worked when he invented the mouse (see the mother of all demos, 85).

We still have vestiges in our computers of that file: in Unix-based systems, such as Linux or macOS X, it can be found in `/etc/hosts` and in Windows-based systems in `\Windows\System32\Drivers\etc\hosts`.

To request a name for an IP, you had to call the SRI during California office hours and talk to the Network Information Center, led by Elizabeth Feinler, so that she could assign a name to an address. However, it became apparent that this would not scale, so Elisabeth and the rest of her team developed the top-level domains we still use today: .com, .edu, .gov, .mil, .org, and .net; thus, opening the door to compartmentalized domain management.

In 1983, Paul Mockapetris and John Postel, inspired by the work of Elisabeth and her team, designed the Domain Name System (DNS), which are online services that perform the automatic function of translating domain names into IP addresses. DNS is the system we use today to translate the domain names we enter into our browser into IP addresses.

However, the Internet is global, and DNS is a large centralized system in the United States. So how do countries agree and trust each other? The answer is simple, they don't, at least not entirely. There have been tensions for over twenty years with ideas such as transferring competencies to the United Nations. Currently, the power is held by an international non-profit organization in California called ICANN.

To maintain its international neutrality, ICANN created a key to open the safes and the hardware that controls the electronic master key to altering the DNS. This key was divided into seven parts; you need at least three of them to access it. The keys (which are smart cards) were distributed to seven carriers in seven countries: Britain, the United States, Burkina Faso, Trinidad and Tobago, Canada, China, and the Czech Republic.

The reason for seven is unknown, but it would not be surprising to discover that it is inspired by Tolkien's seven ring bearers, the seven knights of King Arthur's round table, or even the song *Keeper of the seven keys* by the German metal band Helloween. Of course, we have already seen how computer scientists like to joke (see easter eggs, 28).

The ceremonies to access the key, officially called Root KSK Ceremony, can be visited and are most dramatic. They will generally be given in El Segundo, California, although in case of problems in that location, it could also occur in Culpeper, Virginia.

NEVER GONNA GIVE YOU UP

Veteran users of online services often recommend to newcomers: *don't read the reviews*. What may seem like a whimsical condescension from veterans who need to give advice is a lesson learned with sweat and tears on the battlefields that are the comment areas and internet forums.

Perhaps calling it a *battlefield* is an exaggeration, but there is no doubt that there is a conflict between trolls and unsuspecting users. Trolls are strangers who participate in the forums, intentionally provoking other users to create conflict and uneasiness, either for their enjoyment or for their benefit.

Like so many other things in recent history, we still do not know precisely where the term troll comes from. It is thought to come well from the trolling fishing technique called in English *troll*, in which a lure is slowly dragged from a moving boat, or from the term of the old Norse *troll*, which means giant or demon, we see a demon again in the history of computing! (see ancient greece and the demons of unix, 27).

Trolling was probably born in some BBS or Usenet (see Email predates the Internet, 56), but the first use of which there is sure evidence was in the early '90s on Usenet with the phrase *trolling for newbies*. At that time, it was limited to small antics such as asking in a forum a question that has already been asked on so many other occasions in such a way that any experienced user would not answer. Especially when seeing the veteran's name that the question came from, a new user would enter the conversation, thus wasting his time.

Over time trolling has evolved into different aspects. There is an innocent one of which *rickrolling* can be a good example, which is to present a link with something very tempting to other users and that then will find the link takes them to the music video of the song by Rick Astley, *Never gonna give you up*. Its name seems to come from a previous joke from forums called *4chan* that often embrace trolling. There sometimes, one of those lure links was sent linking to a duck with wheels, something that was called.

In 2008 the rickrolling somehow leaped to real life when thanks to Internet voting, Rick Astley was proposed to the MTV Europe Music Awards for the award of the best artist in history. The trolls got Rick invited to the gala, somehow rickrolling the MTV. In 2006 a troll called a radio show, and instead of talking, he played Never Gonna give you up, which left the DJ speechless, having been rickrolled live on the radio.

> *Never gonna give you up. Never gonna let you down.*
>
> — *Rick Astley, British singer*

Trolling can also fall on the side of cyberbullying. An example of this is *swatting*, a term that describes tricking the police into sending SWAT, their highly militarized special unit, to the home of someone they intend to troll (usually an enemy in some game). Unfortunately, lives have been lost because of this horrible practice, which is heavily punished. Multiple trolls are serving long sentences for these acts.

It is advisable to follow the wisdom often shared as an image to the forums with the phrase: *do not feed the trolls*. Ignore the trolls so that the only ones who waste time are them.

COOKIES

It is virtually impossible to browse without finding a pop-up message showing text similar to *this site uses cookies to improve the experience*. What is this cookie, and to whom do we owe the dubious pleasure of having to accept that a website uses cookies almost every time we browse the Internet?

The term has been used since at least the 70s to define a witness that contains information that is not important to the recipient but must be delivered back to the sender. If we relate it to real life, a good comparison would be when someone goes to the cloakroom and is given a receipt with a number, letters, or anything else. The one who receives it does not need to understand what is written. He must not lose it and deliver it back when he wants his garment returned.

The reason for using the word cookie, which seems to be common in everything related to Unix systems (see the name unix, 26), is difficult to know. However, existing theories speak of similarity with fortune cookies, which keep a message inside that cannot be read; of cookies that are left behind as breadcrumbs to find the way back, or there are even those who venture to relate it to LSD.

We owe the leap from Unix-based operating systems to browsers to Lou Montulli. Before reaching hasty conclusions about Lou and its impact on our user experience, it is relevant to say that cookies are helpful for our experience and that, among other very relevant merits, Lou was one of the drivers of the support in browsers of Gif animations, without which there would be no kittens on the Internet or the famous flame war of Gif vs. Jif (see flame wars, 94).

Lou, one of the founding members of Netscape (see Java and JavaScript. 96), was working there when he was asked to improve the user experience for the shopping cart use case because servers suffered so much from storing too much data.

Lou turned the way he saw the problem around and had the web servers send a cookie, a piece of information that will be stored in the web browser and sent back on each request. It was a great idea. But unfortunately, the problem came later when it began to be used for user tracking purposes. As a result, some countries legislated to force websites to report whether they use cookies and for what purpose.

ENCRYPTION AND THE END OF THE INTERNET

Many of us have felt the need to create secret codes in our childhood. It was essential that our communications with brothers, cousins, and friends were secret, and no one could discover our mischief. Although it might seem like something new and fun at the time, we were not the first to try to hide our communications.

The oldest encryption we know of occurred in 1,500 BC, some thirty-five centuries before our childhood. It was encrypted potter's instructions to make a ceramic glaze. It is interesting to see how the first use was given to protect something with commercial value.

We also have examples of the importance of encrypting our communications between 400 BC and 200 AD. For example, the Kama sutra explained how lovers could send secret messages through encryption.

As for military communications, the story of the German enigma cipher machine is known and how Alan Turing built a machine to decrypt it. It is estimated that it shortened the Second World War by about two years (see we owe you an apology, 79).

In the twenty-first century, encryption appears in almost all of our communications over the Internet. Would we be confident buying online if there were no security guarantees? Would we use the platforms to flirt on the Internet if there was no privacy (see finding love with the internet, 65)?

If encryption stopped working, the twenty-first century would suddenly look like the twentieth century. Of course, many will say that musically this would not be a big problem, but at an industrial, commercial, and even social level, the impact would be gigantic.

That encryption stops working is not necessarily impossible, nor does it have to be very far away. In theory, quantum computing is extremely good at solving certain types of problems, and in that virtue lies a serious problem for our civilization (see quantum supremacy, 12). Sufficiently developed quantum computing would be able to break our current encryption inexorably, and that would probably be the end of the Internet as we know it.

Would there be any way to improve our current encryption to make it resistant to quantum computing? Probably not. But not only is quantum computing being researched to break ciphers, and this is where the hope lies, but quantum encryption is also being investigated. It would represent an encryption so strong that not even another quantum computer could decrypt it. So now, we will have to cross our fingers that quantum encryption arrives before quantum decryption if we want to continue keeping safe our formula for ceramic glazing and the secret communications with our lovers.

THE DEPTHS OF THE INTERNET

In the early '90s, among other events: the Gulf War exploded, Somalia suffered a civil war, in Rwanda, there was a tragic genocide, and China was about to take back Hong Kong. The geopolitical situation could be described as complex if a euphemism were used.

At the time, communications between U.S. intelligence systems and even communications with dissidents, reprisals, and victims of any kind were uncomfortable. Special hardware was needed, and often to communicate, risks had to be taken, which needed to be avoided.

By then, the Internet was already widespread, and the use of the Internet would greatly simplify intelligence communications. Still, the Internet did not offer the degree of military confidentiality that was necessary.

In the mid-'90s, the U.S. Naval Research Laboratory developed a system called *onion routing*. It served to protect communications even from other governments trying to gain access. Later DARPA, a government department that can be considered the Internet's forerunner (see Email predates the Internet, 56), joined the investigation.

> *Ultimately, the dark net is nothing more than a mirror of society. Distorted, magnified, and mutated by the strange and unnatural conditions of life online—but still recognizably us.*
>
> *— Jamie Bartlett, British author, and television presenter*

The name was particularly appropriate because each message sent had different layers. In the heart of the onion, the information that was desired to be sent, and in each of the adjacent layers was only the information necessary for each of the intermediate points of the network so that if someone intercepted a message, he could only see what the next intermediate point would read, not the source or content.

For reasons not entirely known, in 2002, the design of the onion network was made public by the Naval Research Laboratory. According to Roger Dingledine, co-creator of Tor, an open implementation of the onion route, the US could not simply use the routed onion without attracting attention. Anyone would think that whoever used it would be a CIA agent. Therefore, intelligence traffic needed to go unnoticed among other types of traffic.

With the advent of *Tor*, an open-source protocol implementation began what we now call *the dark web (or deep web)*. A dramatic name to describe a part of the network that has barriers to entry because software is needed to enter.

The dark web is often characterized as a network of evil people who use it for evil purposes. Although an anonymous network is very convenient for this type of people, the truth is that there are numerous other uses for these networks, such as free browsing in countries where Internet access is strongly controlled.

If there is a dark web, is there a bright web? Not exactly, but almost. The depths of the network are usually represented by an iceberg, where the deepest peak is the dark web, the tip afloat is the surface web, and all in between is the deep web.

The surface web is the web that we can see and find freely. In other words, anything that can be visited and is findable from a search engine. And the deep web is everything that is not findable from a search engine, for example, private content on social networks or private documents in an online office suite.

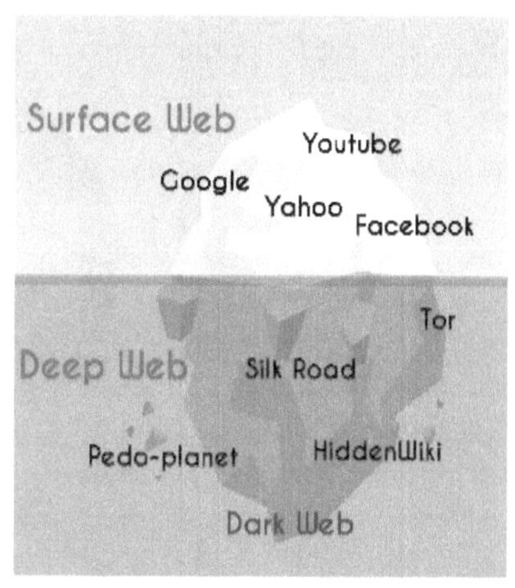

Despite the dramatic names, everything is quite common, right?

FINDING LOVE WITH THE INTERNET

Life finds a way was a phrase immortalized by the character *Ian Malcolm* played by Jeff Goldblum in the classic *Jurassic Park* (1993). As banal as it may seem, flirting is a fundamental part of life and as such, flirting finds a way.

So as new Internet-based technologies came into our homes, the methods of flirting were evolving. For example, in 1988, the Internet Relay Chat (IRC) service was created. With it and a client application, users could connect to rooms where they could talk to other users or send private messages.

The romantic scene remained more or less stable for years. Either you entered chat rooms through IRC or perhaps through some website, which reduced the barrier to entry by not needing to have a specific client installed. Everything changed in 1993 when Gary Kremen had a great idea to design a website to help users find a partner. The site would be called: *match.com*.

The site was released as a free beta (although it would later be paid) in 1995. Gary asked all his friends and employees, including his girlfriend, to create their profiles. Gary became convinced that the site would succeed most unexpectedly, his girlfriend left him for another man she met through the site.

In 1996 the first successful instant messaging system was born; it was called ICQ and was later followed by others such as Microsoft Messenger. These instant messaging systems did not replace Match.com, but they created a whole way to continue online conversations that began in real life.

While flirting online was comfortable and perfectly viable, as Gary's girlfriend showed us, it was just as true that it had some social stigma. Couples often found excuses not to be looked over their shoulder when saying they met over the internet. But, thanks to the movie *You Have an E-Mail* (1998), everything changed when Meg Ryan and Tom Hanks came to rescue netizens from embarrassment by showing that flirting online could be a lovely thing.

In the year 2000, which fortunately was not the apocalypse we thought it was going to be (see the problem of the year 2000, 21), came the first of the great revolutions in this world, the first site that created connections between users using an algorithm that processed the responses of users to a form about their tastes and characteristics.

In 2004 a new leap in terms of user numbers was made when OkCupid and plentyoffish.com appeared, two sites that were (at least in part) free. In 2007 Apple introduced the first iPhone, bringing these sites to the mobile world. But it wasn't until 2009 that Grindr, a flirting social network for gays, showed up. It would be the first application specifically mobile and use mobile qualities such as geopositioning to flirt.

The great explosion of Internet flirting came with simplification. Tinder applied the concept of dragging right or left and focusing on photographs instead of lengthy questionnaires. This grew the number of users exponentially to the numbers we know today.

Who knows if it is thanks to Gary's girlfriend, Tom, and Meg or the entrepreneurs who created these companies, but today you can flirt from anywhere with just a mobile phone.

SEARCH FOR ALIENS FROM HOME

In the XVII, Marin Mersenne, a French monk of the order of the minims (name that refers to the humility of these monks) of well-known friendship with René Descartes, described in a conjecture a

series of numbers that we know today as the Mersenne numbers. *Mersenne numbers* have some unique properties, such as that they may be primes.

Indirectly, these numbers would have a relevant influence on the future search for extraterrestrial intelligence.

In 2018, no less than 430 years after Marin's birth and using his conjecture, Patrick Laroche, a Computer Scientist employed by FedEx in Ocala, Florida, found the most significant prime number known to date. The number is almost 25 million digits long. It takes megabytes to store the number!

How could Patrick find this number before any of the multiple world-scale supercomputers working on the problem?

The answer is that Patrick was not alone. Patrick was one of many volunteers who attached the power of his personal computer to a great joint effort through a *volunteer computing* project. The project is called Great Internet Mersenne Prime Search and was the pioneer software in this type of computing.

In volunteer computing, numerous volunteers through the Internet join, each downloading from a centralized service a portion of the work of a big problem; each one does his part and reports the results to the central service responsible for processing the results.

It might seem that none of these personal computers would become a rival to the great supercomputers; however, knowing that union makes strength, we should have to be able to imagine that the largest supercomputer in the world is a joint effort of volunteers.

For example, in 2020, during the Coronavirus crisis, the distributed computing system: *Folding@home*, which added as a purpose to investigate this virus, reached the record figure of one *exaflop* per second. To understand *exa* let's remember the order of the prefixes of the international system: *kilo, mega, giga, tera, peta* ¡*exa*! Flop, in turn, means floating point operation. This amount is six times more powerful than the largest of its contemporary supercomputers, the *IBM Summit*.

Although GIMPS was the pioneer, the system that made voluntary computing famous was *Seti@Home*. Thanks to it, the waves received by the Arecibo radio telescope of Puerto Rico were analyzed to search for extraterrestrial intelligence.

> *I think the most certain sign that there is intelligent life out there in the universe is that no one has tried to contact us.*
>
> —*Bill Watterson, cartoonist who created Calvin and Hobbes*

Today the project is paused and has been succeeded in fame both by the Folding@home as mentioned earlier, and by the BOINC project of the same creators who Seti@Home, and which allows collaboration with various scientific projects using only one program.

Just in case, it's worth mentioning that the Electronic Frontier Foundation offers a prize of $150,000 for the first to find a prime with 100,000,000 digits.

PEER-TO-PEER NETWORKS

Shawn Fanning did not have a simple childhood, the son of a single mother with money always being a problem. His neighborhood was rough, and he was rather shy. Sean used to spend the afternoons at home. His mother turned to his younger brother, John, to help and inspire his nephew, something John did dedicatedly.

When Shawn was still in high school, he received a gift from his uncle John, who was professionally dedicated to the world of video games. It was an Apple Macintosh 512+. John didn't have high hopes, thinking it would just be just another escape route for Sean, but he was soon surprised by how Shawn learned to use it with an intensity and speed he hadn't seen in anyone before.

With his computer and an Internet connection, Shawn discovered IRC (see finding love with the internet, 65). Inside IRC, he found the most clandestine corners where he could learn hacking techniques and download programs and music in MP3 format.

As early as 1998, Shawn was among many newcomers to Northeastern University in Boston, Massachusetts. In the first year, it had a revelation what if there was a better way to download MP3 than to go to the most dubious corners of the Internet? What if the record industry was wrong in selling plastic records with 12 songs, of which only one was good?

He talked about it with someone who had known such places online, Sean Parker, who at 15 had already caught the attention of the FBI for his hacks and had to serve services to the community for it. Sean loved the idea, and together they began to program one of the programs that have had the most impact on their own in the world; whether this positive or negative impact is up to each one.

Shawn and Sean created Napster. A program that allowed downloading songs in MP3 format in a somewhat peculiar way, instead of reaching a centralized server, which would be challenging if there were many users and because it would be an easy victim of any legal litigation, they created a network where users could share the songs they had directly, so Napster's role was quite ambiguous in the transaction.

These types of networks are called peer-to-peer or P2P networks. They were complicated to stop legally since it was the users themselves who shared the files. In some countries, users were even protected by laws that allowed them to share if there was no profit motive.

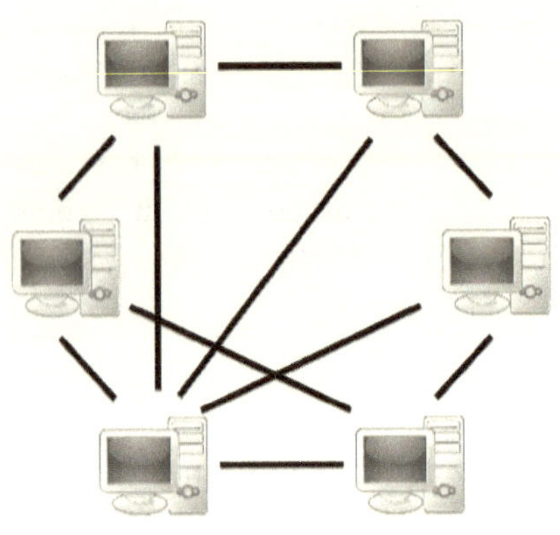

As if this were not enough, the technology could scale very quickly since most of the work was done by the users' computers, which were widespread worldwide. In a way, it could be said that P2P networks are a kind of voluntary computer network (see search for aliens from home, 67), but instead of sharing computing power, it is about sharing files.

> *I think that's what happened to the record business when Napster came around. The industry rejected what was happening instead of accepting it as change.*
>
> —*Jay-Z, American rapper*

Napster was not the first P2P network, there was at least one previous one called *hotline*, but it was undoubtedly the network that has had the most significant impact. According to some members of the record industry, Napster created a whole generation of music consumers who expected music to be free, which made the industry stagger and change forever.

For years record labels chose to fight legally and try to maintain the model they used for years. They eventually beat Napster, but a change was already underway, and the music industry never returned to what it was.

After Napster, Shawn founded multiple startups. Sean was Facebook's first president and today is an investor who holds shares in companies like Spotify. Justin Timberlake famously portrayed Sean in the film *The Social Network* (2010).

THE INTERNET'S MEMORY

We know of laws that governed ancient Babylon because a carved stone, the code of Hammurabi, reached our times. We know the gods of ancient Egypt, among other reasons, from the scrolls that came to us. From ancient Greece, we know its politics from its writings, and from Rome, we have known its civil engineering thanks to their imperishable infrastructures.

What do all these sources of wisdom have in common? First, they are analog, live in the real world, and do not require special tools to be used. In addition, they cannot simply disappear from the world overnight; from an extinct civilization will remain sculptures, frescoes, cemeteries, and bridges, among others.

If we leap into modern times, where our knowledge has fundamentally become digital, can we be confident that there will be a legacy of our culture for the future?

To find out, you can try to access our contemporary knowledge. For example, in the '90s, the most famous web hosting service was *Geo-Cities*, which has now disappeared. Do we know today what any of the many websites hosted there looked like? Do we know what was in the private content sections of places like the retired Google Wave or Google Videos? Can you play a video game with strong copy protections written for a defunct platform?

Brewster Kahle, an Internet activist, and a computer scientist, wondered about these same questions. Brewster had a considerable impact on the Internet by co-founding WAIS Inc., which he sold to

America Online. In addition, Brewster founded Alexa Internet, the famous traffic measurement site, and sold it to Amazon. But what he did afterward has had a much higher value from the point of view of the general interest.

Brewster founded The Internet Archive, a non-profit organization responsible for storing as much content as possible and its different versions over time. He archives music, games, and videos, and one of his most famous projects is the Wayback Machine.

The Wayback Machine periodically visits and stores almost all of the surface web (see the depths of the internet, 63) and allows you to see the old versions of the sites just by entering their address. It is the most fun to see what online newspapers or the best-known web services looked like years ago.

Don't miss it

The headquarters of the Internet Archive is located in San Francisco, California, and usually offers free tours. The building is an old de-sacralized church. In the main hall, you can find ceramic figures of the Internet Archive employees, collaborators, and inspirers, such as Ted Nelson and Aaron Swartz, created by artist Nuala Creed.

Geniuses

The people who are crazy enough to think they can change the world are the ones who do.

— Steve Jobs, Co-Founder of Apple Inc.

THE FRUSTRATED FIRST COMPUTER

Charles Babbage was born in England at the end of the eighteenth century and was considered curmudgeonly stubborn and a mathematics genius.

When Charles found something he didn't like, he didn't just angrily criticize it but also tried to fix it. And so, it was with the books of tables, which contained tables of trigonometric calculations, tides, interest rates, gravity, multiplications, logarithms, and so on.

These books sometimes contained errata from a computer error, which, at the time, was a human with a trade called *computer*. It was not a machine. And even when the calculations had been made and revised to perfection, errors were often introduced into the printing press when preparing the plates.

Therefore, Charles decided to design a machine to do calculations mechanically and called it the *difference engine*. To seduce potential investors, Charles built with his resources a partial version, which today we would consider a demo version, and called it *the beautiful fragment*. Then, he frequented the meetings of high society, showing the fragment to anyone who might be interested. In one of them, he met someone who would later be instrumental: Ada Lovelace (see the first programmer, 75).

The differential machine could calculate polynomial functions, so it was quite a breakthrough, but it was not yet as generalist as he wanted. In addition, with the construction techniques of Victorian gears, building it was becoming a struggle.

Instead of giving up, Charles doubled down on his efforts and designed a general-purpose computing machine and designed the first computer no less than 100 years ahead of history.

He called this new invention the analytical engine. It contained a part called the mill that would be equivalent to the modern CPU and also has a storage area, that is, what we would call memory today.

This mechanical machine was given the programs the same way they would be given to the first electronic machines of the future, with punched cards. However, for the output, it had a printer! The first printer ever created. This was due to Charles' obsession with avoiding the transcription errors he hated so much, which occurred in 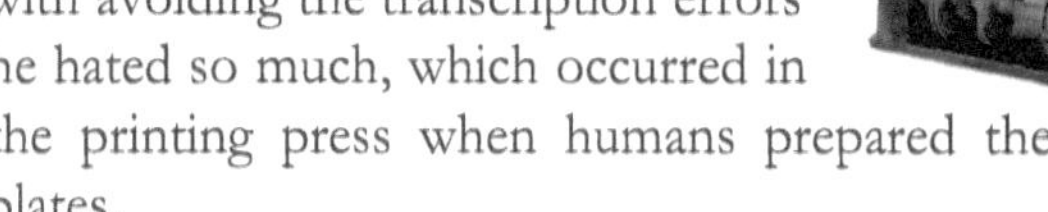 the printing press when humans prepared the plates.

Unfortunately, Victorian engineering was not advanced enough to create this machine, so it was left only as a theoretical exercise. Therefore, whether an unmanufactured machine is really the first computer can be questioned. Be that as it may, this machine allowed the first program to be written, regardless of whether it was executed or not.

Don't miss it

The Science Museum in London has on display a Babbage machine that he built for the two-hundredth anniversary of Babbage's birth. In addition, the museum built a second unit for one of the project's benefactors: Nathan Myhrvold, who was CTO of Microsoft. He, in turn, temporarily lent his machine to the California Computer Museum in 2008, and this loan ended up lasting almost a decade. Today it is in Seattle in private hands.

THE FIRST PROGRAMMER

Ada was born Augusta Ada Byron. His parents were George Gordon Byron, Lord Byron, a notable English poet, and Anne Isabella Milbanke.

For lovers of poetry, it is known that Lord Byron was what today we would call a rock star. Lovers, extravagant pets, and as many drinks as possible were his way of life. George abandoned his wife just weeks after she gave birth to Ada and only a few months after their marriage. His first sentence to Ada was: *Oh! What an implement of torture have I acquired in you!* He never saw Ada again after abandoning her.

Ada had a high-level and rigorous scientific education. Her mother intended to take her away from poetry to keep her afar from her father's madness in case she had inherited it.

At 18, Ada met Charles Babbage (see the frustrated first computer, 74) at a society event. Since then, she maintained frequent correspondence with Charles, who nicknamed her *the enchantress of numbers.*

> *A new, a vast, and a powerful language is developed for the future use of analysis, in which to wield its truths so that these may become of more speedy and accurate practical application for the purposes of mankind...*
>
> *—Ada Lovelace, the first programmer*

Ada met William King, Earl of Lovelace, whom she married. As was customary then, she took the name and title of her husband, becoming Ada King Countess of Lovelace, or as we usually refer to her: Ada Lovelace. After a period away from mathematics due to the birth of her three children, she decided to return to her mathematical studies, and boy did she return!

At that time, Babbage had barely defined what would be the analytical machine without getting to build it. Because of his peculiar personality, Babbage did not make his machine public in England but accepted an invitation to give a lecture in Italy. There he spoke about his analytical machine, and the engineer Luigi Menabrea, who later became the Italian prime minister, wrote an article about it.

Ada knew of the existence of that article and decided to translate it, but while translating it, she decided she could improve it and began adding notes to the side. Those notes grew until Ada created the first computer program. Of course, Babbage would have been the first programmer to have created programs to test the design of his machine, but Ada was the first to create a program, thinking of the machine as a computer and not as a glorified calculator.

For Babbage, Ada was fascinating because she saw his machine in a completely different way than others (even himself). Where others saw a calculator, Ada could see text, images, and music being processed. Ada wrote in 1843: *the machine could compose elaborate and scientific pieces of music of any complexity and measure.*

Today Ada is generally recognized as the first programmer and, without any doubt, the first to have a vision of what modern computing would be. In her honor, multiple things have been named, from robots with artificial intelligence to a programming language, and she is a symbol of gender equality in computer science.

THE FIRST COMPUTER BUILT

Since his youth, the young Konrad Zuse, born in Berlin in 1910, had proven to be an inventor. He created a fruit vending machine that returned the change and even created, with a Stabil mechanical kit, something similar to a construction kit from Mecano, a coal loading crane. Stabil gave Konrad a certificate of honor for this invention.

With such concerns, it was only a matter of time before Konrad studied civil engineering. As a student, Konrad hated the routine statistical calculations that he had to perform, which consumed so many hours that he could use for more rewarding tasks.

When he started working in an aeronautical company, analyzing vibration fatigue in the fuselages in wings of airplanes, this hatred was exacerbated and pushed him to leave work and start his adventure to try to end the loss of time because of tedious calculations.

In his parent's living room, perhaps beginning with the trend of using space in the parent's house that will find an echo in the pioneers of Silicon Valley, he began the creation of a kind of programmable super calculator that he called the Z1. To build it, he used mechanical components since Zuse did not yet have much knowledge of electronics. However, in the Z1, Zuse already used very advanced concepts such as stored programs, in this case in 35mm film tape, a control unit, and an arithmetic unit.

In 1938 the Z1 was started for the first time and performed the calculation of a 3x3 matrix, and it worked! However, as expected, the machine was composed of thousands of mechanical parts and often failed. The Z1 and its blueprints were destroyed in Allied aerial bombardment during World War II. However, in 1980 Konrad and engineering students began work on reconstruction and completed it in 1989. Fortunately, the reconstruction can be visited in Berlin at the Deutsches Technikmuseum.

> *There is a replica of this model (Z1) in the Museum of Traffic and Technology in Berlin. Back then it didn't work well, and in that sense, the replica is very reliable and doesn't work well either.*
>
> *—Konrad Zuse, German engineer*

Konrad created the Z2 by improving the design of the Z1 using this time electromechanical relays, typically used in telephony, to implement the control unit. As a result, they made it more reliable, and thanks to this newly acquired reliability, he got funds to create the Z3.

Finally, in 1941, Konrad introduced the Z3, the first calculating machine that worked through a control program and, therefore, the first computer ever built. Again, a lifetime of work and dedication only to stop doing the tedious accounts he did at his first job!

Don't miss it

The Konrad Zuse Museum in Hünfeld, just over an hour from Frankfurt, has an extensive collection of devices created by Zuse, including a reconstruction of the Z3 by Raul Rojas and Horst Zuse, Son of Konrad. In addition, the German Museum of Technology in Berlin has a reconstruction of the Z1 led by Zuse himself.

WE OWE YOU AN APOLOGY

For Alan Turing, born in London in 1912, mathematics was everything. From childhood, he developed excellent skills and an affection for mathematics and learning.

When he was 14 years old and joined Sherborne Boarding School in Dorset, his first day coincided with a general strike. Such was his love of learning that Alan covered the 96.5 km that separated him from the boarding school by bicycle. His sports skills were not limited to this; he almost reached the Olympics as a runner in 1948, but an unfortunate hip dislocation prevented him from doing so.

He was admitted to Kings College, Cambridge, and there he decided to solve one of the great problems of mathematics, the so-called: *Entcsheidungsproblem* (in English, the decision problem) proposed by the German David Hilbert, no less than one of the greatest mathematicians of the nineteenth and twentieth centuries.

While running along the edge of the Camb River in Cambrige, to solve the *Entcsheidungsproblem* he came up with the idea of designing what he called the *Logical Computing Machine* that later came to be called the Turing machine. While the machine was a theoretical exercise, it undoubtedly laid the foundations of modern computing. Modern programming languages always seek to prove that they are Turing complete, meaning they can do the same thing a Turing machine can do.

Alan's contributions to computing do not end there. He went on to theorize about artificial intelligence, defining the Turing test (see I'm not a robot, 23).

He became a national hero, although this was not known until after his death because he was classified since he devised the machine that managed to break the encryption of the famous German enigma machine. This breakthrough is considered to have shortened the Second World War, thus saving countless lives.

Anyone would think that their country would give Alan a hero's treatment. However, not only was it not so, but after an investigation in his apartment, after he had been robbed, it was discovered that he was homosexual. Something illegal at the time. He was forced to choose between chemical castration or prison, as well as no longer being able to work for national security. Public derision was guaranteed. Alan chose chemical castration.

Finally, Alan bit an apple with traces of cyanide, most likely intentionally, thus tragically taking his own life at 41.

> *If a machine is expected to be infallible, it cannot also be intelligent.*
>
> *—Alan Turing, British mathematician*

In 2009, 55 years after his death from a public petition, UK Prime Minister Gordon Brown issued a statement apologizing on behalf of his government for the treatment Alan Turing received during his last years. Although three years later, David Cameron's government denied him a pardon, it was finally granted by order of Queen Elizabeth II on 24 December 2013.

For years it was thought that the Apple logo of the multicolored bitten apple paid homage to Alan for being an apple, being bitten, and having colors very similar to the rainbow flag. However, Rob Janoff, the creator of the logo, denied it. The rainbow flag was created after the Apple logo, and the bite was only there as a size reference to differentiate the apple from a cherry.

PROGRAMMING FOR EVERYONE

When little Grace Hopper, born in New York in 1906, she was only seven years old and disassembled devices just for the pleasure of understanding how they worked. One day her mother realized that Grace had dismantled the seven alarm clocks they had in her house and punished her with just being able to disassemble one. But, grace's voracious curiosity would not be stopped so quickly.

And it was to the point that Grace graduated in mathematics and physics at Vassar College and got a master's degree and a doctorate in mathematics at Yale. Once she completed her studies, she was a devoted teacher to her students at Vassar College. Her answer to the question of what was her most outstanding achievement not related to computer science is well-known; she replied: *the young people I educated.*

By then, World War II had begun. Hopper wanted to do her part, so she joined a program in which she was allowed to do jobs beyond nursing or management duties. She attended the naval cadet school for women and was called to collaborate with the Mark computer series at Harvard with the rank of lieutenant.

The first of these, the Mark I, partly inspired by Babbage's analytical engine (see the frustrated first computer, 74), was the first electro-mechanical computer in the United States. She and her colleagues Richard Milton Bloch and Robert Campbell formed a group of computer pioneers who created programs for the machine, becoming some of the first programmers to run programs on a computer and some of the first programmers of modern computing.

> *It is better to ask for forgiveness than to ask for permission*
>
> *—Grace Hopper, computer scientist*

Grace was an untamed soul who saw opportunities where others saw problems. At that time, computers were programmed in a machine code very close to the machine. Therefore, you had to be a student of the particular machine to be able to use it. To make computing closer to everyone, Grace created the first *compiler* (in fact, she also coined the term itself), a program capable of translating source code (see free software, 20) easy for humans to understand into computer-executable machine code.

And this is not all. Among her other numerous achievements, she also has the creation of the first cross-platform programming language: COBOL. In 1960 a COBOL program was compiled and run on a UNIVAC II computer and an RCA 501 computer. The relevance of COBOL today is such that during the COVID-19 pandemic in 2020, in New Jersey, COBOL developer volunteers were requested to fix the unemployment insurance systems since it could not cope with such a rise in demand.

She is beloved not only for her multiple academic and professional achievements. Grace was an overwhelming personality. Today she represents a role model for young programmers around the world.

Don't miss it

The Mark I that Grace worked with was partially disassembled. However, today we can still see a renovated Mark I at the Harvard University Science Center.

THE ATYPICAL GENIUS

Neumann János Lajos was born in beautiful Budapest, still part of the Austro-Hungarian Empire, in 1903. To get an idea of János' talent for mathematics, we can read what his friend and schoolmate from a higher grade, later nothing less than a Nobel Prize in Physics, Eugene Wigner, said about him: *Having met János, I realized the difference between a leading mathematician and me.*

His family emigrated to Germany because of the political turbulence of World War I Hungary and studied in Berlin. He used to alternate his life between Germany, where he was an associate professor, and the United States, as Princeton often invited him to attend. However, his mind changed with the rise to power of the Nazi party in Germany, and he emigrated to the United States.

While in Germany, given his wealthy origin, he began to be called Jon von Neumann. In the United States, he was John. John's personality could fill an entire room; everyone loved spending time with him. His home somehow became Princeton's cultural and entertainment center, where brilliant minds and personalities conversed and pollinated ideas with each other. His wife, at the time, said of him: *John can count anything but calories*. He was the complete opposite of the archetype of a shy scientist.

> *I have known a great many intelligent people in my life. I knew Max Planck, Max von Laue, and Werner Heisenberg. Paul Dirac was my brother-in-law; Leo Szilard and Edward Teller have been among my closest friends; and Albert Einstein was a good friend, too. And I have known many of the brightest younger scientists. But none of them had a mind as quick and acute as Jancsi von Neumann. I have often remarked this in the presence of those men, and no one ever disputed me.*
>
> *—Eugene Wigner, Nobel Prize in Physics*

At that time, John was mainly dedicated to quantum physics, in which he was co-responsible for significant advances such as quantum logic, on which quantum computing is fundamentally based (see quantum supremacy, 12). He invited Alan Turing (see we owe you an apology, 79) to be his associate professor, but perhaps because Johnnie was not yet fully committed to computing or, as many claim, because of Alan's patriotic duty to help his country in World War II, the offer was declined.

When the evolution of events in World War II and Nazi scientific progress made the American government realize the need to be the first in nuclear science, the Manhattan Project was created. It had some of the most influential minds of the time, such as Enrico Fermi, Robert Oppenheimer, Albert Einstein, and Richard Feynman. But, of course, John was also part of the team.

It is said that in the Manhattan Project, sometimes they had to do a calculation, and Feynman did it with a desktop calculator, Fermi with a small slide rule that he always carried on him, and von Neumann, in his head. John used to win, and it was remarkable how close the three results always were.

The project was not his only contribution in search of an Allied victory in the war. John also worked for the University of Pennsylvania at ENIAC, a vacuum tube-based computer that operated in a decimal system and was used to calculate ballistic trajectories. To get an idea of the complexity of the computer, the temperature in the room rose to 50 degrees Celsius (around 120 Fahrenheit) when it was put to work. There was also an urban legend that in Philadelphia, blackouts happened when the ENIAC came into operation due to its consumption of 160 kW.

However, ENIAC came somewhat late for this purpose as it was completed in 1946, and the war ended in September 1945. However, John found a way to rewire this machine to make calculations that would be useful for the atomic bomb, thus somehow turning it into a general-purpose machine.

At the war's end, several countries had different computer development projects, some binary, others decimal, some electronic, others electromechanical, some general-purpose other specific purposes. Once again, at the University of Pennsylvania, they took it very seriously to move forward in this direction by creating the successor to the ENIAC, which would be called EDVAC, a role model for posterity.

The university invited all those interested in computing to spend a summer researching. There, numerous figures gathered and designed a computer. The general architecture was described by John von Neumann and is known as the von Neumann architecture. This architecture is precisely the one that today's computers still use to this day.

It is difficult to summarize all von Neumann's contributions to science but to understand their relevance, it would suffice to mention that in addition to the theory of the self-reproducible automaton (see viruses, worms, trojans, and other bad weeds, 25) and the Von Neumann architecture, on which all our computers run today, he also created quantum logic, that defines how the computers of the future will work.

Don't miss it

Unfortunately, from the EDVAC, one of the most influential computers in history, we have almost nothing left. Only a few circuits remain in the Smithsonian's National Museum of American History, and other pieces are kept at the University of Pennsylvania.

From the ENIAC, the University of Pennsylvania has on display four of the original forty panels in the Moore School Building.

THE MOTHER OF ALL DEMOS

Douglas Engelbart grew up on a small farm just outside Portland, Oregon. Although his father was a radio amateur, he did not inherit his passion for technology. His life was a simple rural life, as he tells in the interview of the oral history series of the Museum of the History of Computing in California.

When he arrived at the university, there was a lot of excitement around a novel technology called *radar*. So he decided he wanted to study something related to it because it seemed like something new and exciting.

When he was called to World War II, he was assigned as a telecommunications maintenance technician. They embarked him in the port of San Francisco on his way to Oceania front with the luck that when he had barely left and was passing under the Bay Bridge, the captain looked out on the deck and shouted: Japan has surrendered! He could then see and hear San Francisco erupt in jubilation. So after a somewhat quieter military service than he expected, he returned and married.

However, shortly after getting engaged, he realized that he had no goals in life that went beyond a good job, getting married, and living happily. According to himself, with great naivety, by the simplicity of his country boy mind, he reasoned that his goal in life was to make the world a better place by making the collective human intellect better through computers. This was when computers were seen as little more than tools for processing numbers.

Finally, after some professional changes, he dedicated himself to his goal at the Stanford Research Institute in Menlo Park, California. There, he began researching what I call the ON-Line System (NLS) with ARPA funding. There he and his team, among which Bill English should be highlighted, designed the first mouse that they called *XY position indicator for a display system*. That first mouse had the cable coming out from behind and that someone from that team, who exactly nobody remembers, ended up nicknaming it mouse.

At a conference in San Francisco, Douglas and his team demonstrated the mouse and many other inventions and practically defined the fundamentals of modern personal computing: windows, graphics, hypertext, video conferencing, the first-word processor, version control, and others. The demo is so legendary and ahead of its time that it has been dubbed *the mother of all demos*. It is straightforward to find it online, and even today, it is impressive to see. But unfortunately, he was so ahead of his time that despite their big ovation, he didn't directly influence the industry, at least immediately.

> *If Xerox had known what it had and had taken advantage of its real opportunities, it could have been as big as IBM plus Microsoft plus Xerox combined and the largest high-technology company in the world.*
>
> —*Steve Jobs, Co-Founder of Apple Inc.*

However, by chance of fate, his partner Bill English and part of his team ended up working at Xerox. There they worked on designing a computer called the Xerox alto, following the lines presented in the mother of all demos. Then, one day, a certain Steve Jobs from the small startup Apple Inc visited them. When Steve saw the mouse and the window system, he started jumping around the room, screaming, *Why don't you do anything with this? This is wonderful. It's revolutionary.* The rest is history.

Programming

PROGRAMMING BY PUNCHING HOLES

In 1789, by constitutional mandate, the United States became the first country to conduct population censuses periodically. The constitution stated that they were to be done every ten years, which was perfectly feasible initially, with only four million Americans.

However, in 1890, just a century later, the population already amounted to sixty-four million. Estimates indicated that a census would take longer than the decade they had of time, so a new census would begin before the previous one was completed.

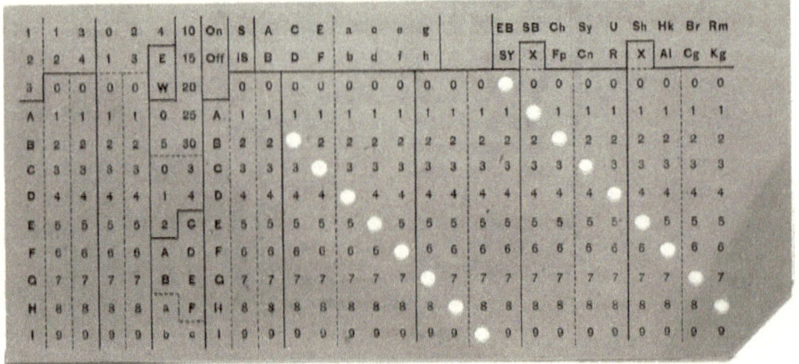

The government called a competition to find a solution. The best proposal came from the mining engineer and ingenious inventor Herman Hollerith. Herman noticed that census questions could be answered with a yes or no. This gave him the idea of using some pieces of cardboard, which we know today as *Hollerith cards*, which would indicate yes or no depending on how they were punched.

These cards had that shape for being counted automatically, dramatically speeding up the count. The machine in charge of doing it was *Hollerith's machine*. The machine had a kind of plate with needles armed with springs. By putting the card underneath, the perforations would let through the needles reaching a mercury base, thus closing a circuit that would allow accounting.

These machines would later be adapted for army health statistics and to prepare the agricultural census. Later Herman oriented his machines to accounting and business. The importance of these cards is such that after merging his company with three others, the company

Programming

International Business Machines was created, perhaps better known by its acronym: IBM.

It should be clarified that Charles Babbage intended to use a similar technique in his analytical machine (see the frustrated first computer, 74). Still, it was never built, and in 1801 the French inventor Joseph Marie Jacquard managed to automate a loom similarly. That said, Herman used the cards to process information, that is, the strictest sense of the word *computer*.

The first computers did not yet have hard drives, so they received both the data and the program in punched format, either as punched cards or later in perforated tapes, which we can imagine as a cinema movie roll but with perforations.

The programming was done on something similar to a typewriter, but instead of writing on a sheet of paper, it wrote on a punched card. Each card typically represented a command leaving a stack of cards inserted into the computer at the end.

If a mistake were made, it would not be known until it was executed, possibly days later, and be careful that the stack of cards does not fall because if they lose their order, it is almost impossible to reorder them. Each programmer has their trick to not lose the order, from numbering them to drawing diagonal lines on the sides of the card stack so that it would be easy to reconstruct the stack.

This will almost certainly surprise any modern programmer where the integrated development environment does wonders to help them complete their task. In addition, if anyone was tempted to make a bad joke by saying that real men enter the information with punch cards, it should be clarified that almost all the operators of the drilling machines were women.

HELLO WORLD

In 1972, the revered Canadian programmer Brian Kernighan, author among many other achievements of the famous C K&R manual and the Unix utility AWK (the K comes in fact, from his surname Kernighan), wrote a tutorial on how to program in the programming language B (precursor of the widespread C) the following code:

```
main( ) {
    extern a, b, c;
    putchar(a); putchar(b); putchar(c);
putchar('!*n');
}
a 'hell';
b 'o, w';
c 'orld';
```

The only thing this little program did was write in the *hello, world*! Later this example was taken to the most famous book written about C, which gave birth to the most widespread tradition among programmers: the *Hello World*.

Since then, almost every programmer has used hello world when learning a new programming language. If you plan to learn a language, almost certainly, the first example you stumble upon in your manual, tutorial, or course is the hello world.

The tradition is so deep-rooted that there is even a website dedicated to collecting different versions of Hello World since 1994. At the time of writing this edition, they have hello world in 593 programming languages and 78 human languages!

FOOBAR

Perhaps one of the most confusing moments for someone learning to code is the first time they read code written by someone else. If the code's author is old school, it is quite possible that he called a variable *foobar*. However, it could also appear as *waldo*, if this person studied at Harvard, *zxc* if he did it in Cambridge, *pippo* if he comes from Italy, *aap* for Holland, etc.

Going to an internet search engine may not help if your first result tells you it is a *metasyntactic variable*. This ornate name indicates that it is a variable whose identity is unimportant and is only used to prove a concept. So, for example, in an article, someone may need to add two variables that are not important because what matters is the function of the sum, so that they could use the variables foobar and foobaz, two metasyntactic variables, in such a way that all our attention is focused on the sum function.

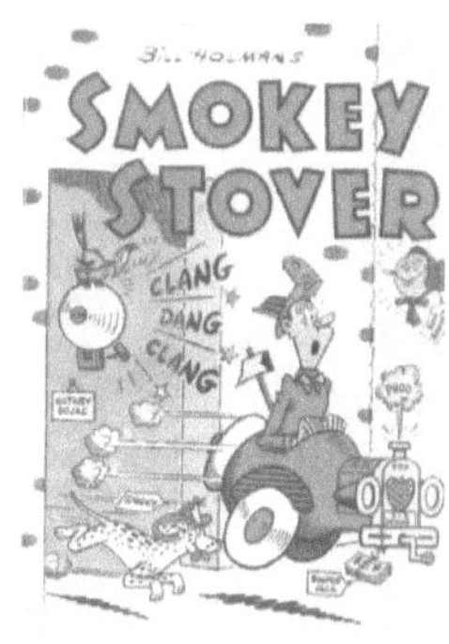

The origin of the expression is not entirely known. It may have military origin coming from FUBAR (Fouled Up Beyond All Recognition), from the comic Smokey Stover, invented by the MIT student association called Tech Model Railroad Club, or even simply coming from the German furchtbar (terrible in English).

DEBUGGING WITH A RUBBER DUCKY

Imagine this situation. We have a programmer who spends the day writing a very complex piece of code, and there is something that does not end up working. So he finally decides to ask his partner for help.

Just a few words after starting to explain the problem, without the partner getting to say a word, he realizes the solution and says to the partner: Oh! It doesn't matter. I already realized what was wrong.

The next day the same thing happens again with another problem. And on the third day yet again, but with one caveat. This time the partner gives him a rubber ducky and says, don't tell me anything. First, tell the rubber ducky, and you will see how he helps you solve the problem.

The moral of this story is that using the technique of Rubber ducky debugging, that is, telling another being, even inanimate, the nature of your problem helps us to put our thoughts in order and often even to find the cause of our problem.

This technique was first described in the highly influential book *The Pragmatic Programmer*, which is often used as a textbook in universities despite being only a book of tricks and tips to be a better programmer.

On the other hand, you would think that if the rubber duckies are so smart, why don't we put them to program instead of us humans?

ADDING A DUCK

According to the story transmitted by word of mouth by the employees of the company Interplay, that was eventually collected in the New Programming Jargon of Jeff Atwood. While the famous chess game *Battle Chess* was being developed, which most veterans will perhaps remember for its spectacular animated characters. There

was a producer, a role similar to that of a project manager, who used to ask for changes to the artists' work so he could feel that he contributed his two cents.

One of the animators, tired of making unnecessary corrections to make the producer feel better when making the queen animations, put a duck flying over his head, placing it carefully so that the duck and the queen did not overlap. Hence, it was effortless to remove it from the animation.

When presenting the animations to the producer, he said: *it's all good, just one thing, take the duck away.*

Today in programming jargon, making a duck refers to deliberately introducing something you know should be removed to protect something that should not be removed.

It's the second time a duck has saved a programmer in this book. Why would it be?

Other terms of the New Programming Jargon

🖥 **Heisenbug**, a bug with some kind of uncertainty principle that makes it disappear or alter its characteristics when studied.

🖥 **Loch Ness monster** bug, is a bug that has only been seen by one person, and there is no way to reproduce it.

🖥 **Hydra code**, is code that cannot be fixed. Like the Hydra of legend, every new fix introduces two new bugs.

🖥 **Baklava code**, code divided into too many layers of little value, which forces you to remember each of them when studying the code.

🖥 **Smurf name convention**, when almost all entities in the code are prefixed with a name as the Smurfs did: `SmurfAccountView`, `SmurfAccountDTO` or `SmurfAccountController`.

IMAGE PROCESSING AND PLAYBOY

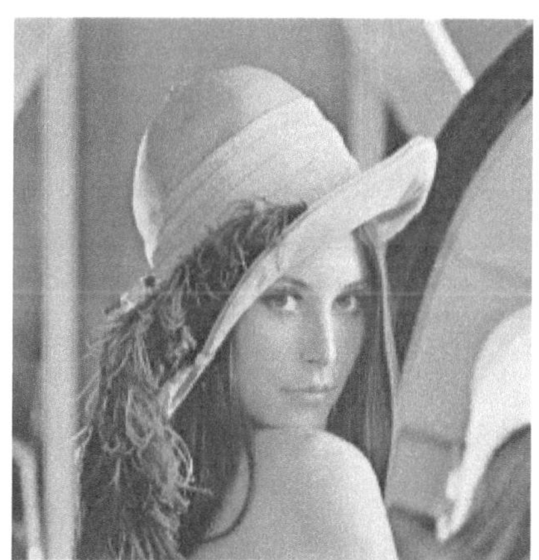

At one point in June or July 1973, Alexander Sawchuk, an adjunct professor at USC in Los Angeles, along with a student and the lab manager, were looking for an image they could use for an image processing conference. They had grown tired of their old images from the early '60s. Instead, they wanted something shiny, with different textures and colors, and if possible, that had in it a human face.

possible, that had in it a human face.

At that moment, someone found a Playboy magazine as if by magic. They cut out a piece of the center drop-down to only show the model's hat, face, and shoulders and scanned it.

That image ended up being used in numerous articles on image processing and became one of the most used images in the history of computing; some may say it is the *Hello World* of image processing (see hello world, 89). In fact, the scanning of this photo has been described by technology review as one of the most important events in the history of electronic imaging.

The image was named Lena, after the model that appears, Lena Söderberg. Although it is still used today, its use is being widely questioned for representing sexism in the sciences.

THE WEISSMAN SCORE

In 2014, HBO offered audiences a hilarious TV series about Silicon Valley. So real that Silicon Valley it was said that it seemed more like a documentary rather than a comedy.

They even shot the general shots of a party in which they wanted Eric Schmidt (former CEO of Google) to appear and went to ask him to shoot scenes in which he would appear. When someone showed him what they had already shot, Eric said: I have been at that party (thinking he had been there).

No detail of realism was left to chance, including the score they used to measure the quality of the compression systems: *the Weissman score*.

Such a score was paramount to the script and plot of the series, yet nothing like this existed in the real world. So, the producers of the series contacted Tsachy Weissman, a professor at Stanford University, who, along with his student Vinith Mishra created the scoring system by naming it in honor of the professor.

In 2017, the score was used by Dropbox in the real world to demonstrate its progress in lossless compression.

FLAME WARS

An in-depth study of the programmer's psyche is yet to be done. In the meantime, we can only look at the short history of computing and assume the nature of this beautiful creature.

One of the facts that outstand when observing the herds of programmers in their natural habitat, which would be a room full of pizza and soda, although any online forum also works, is that for almost every topic, they seem to organize themselves into two frontally opposed groups in what they call the flame wars.

> *In a room full of top software designers, if two agree on the same thing, that's a majority.*
>
> — *Dr. Bill Curtis, computer scientist*

A flame war consists of a war on two sides that will tend never to end and where logic and education are usually optional. Examples of flame wars in full development would be:

Tabs versus spaces, two sides are fighting fiercely to find out the best tabulation method in the source code of programs. Proponents of the tab say it uses fewer characters, those in favor of spaces that look the same in any editor.

Little endian versus big endian, the interesting thing about this war is that it is fought by CPU designers, a highly specialized underworld. In it, they try to decide the correct order of the bytes for the CPU instructions.

Gif vs. jif, debating how the name of the famous animated image format is pronounced. According to the author of the format itself, *jif* is the correct pronunciation, which is in itself a solid argument. On the other hand, President Barack Obama gave his official position in June 2014, its *gif* with a hard G.

ESOTERIC PROGRAMMING LANGUAGES

We often see programming as a very serious form of engineering full of rules, calculations, tests, architectures, and other complications.

For many programmers, however, it is not only a job but also a hobby. We are talking about such a big science with so many potential uses that during the day, a developer can spend hours developing a banking program to get home at night and still feel like programming, only this time, it could be a controller of a mini-submarine, a program to fulfill the dream of having a startup or perhaps a PC game.

And suppose the programmer in question, in addition to wanting to continue with his hobby, turns out to be an inveterate prankster. In that case, he may want to create an esoteric language.

There is some form of secret competition between the creators of esoteric languages, in which it is valued that languages are at the same time straightforward but very difficult to understand, virtues that might seem opposite. Still, that esoteric languages amply show us that they are not.

Two good examples of esoteric languages would be *whitespace*, a language that only uses white space and tabs to be written. It is so decidedly esoteric that you can't print the code because you wouldn't see anything. The other would be *brainfuck* which only uses symbols to express itself. The following example is a simple *hello world*, although it looks more like gibberish!

```
+++++++[>++++[>++>+++>+++>+<<<<-]>+>+>->>+[<]<-]>>.>-
--.+++++++..  +++.>>.<-.<.+++.------.---------.>>+.>++.
```

JAVA AND JAVASCRIPT

Although it is difficult to imagine today, the first Internet browser, created in 1990 by Sir Tim Berners-lee, only worked in text mode.

It wasn't until 1993 that Mark Andreessen created the Mosaic browser, using funds from the High-Performance Computing Act, which Al Gore signed. Remember Al Gore's famous meme saying he created the Internet?

Mark later moved to California, where he co-founded Netscape, and in just two years, the Netscape browser dominated an 80% market share.

At this point, the web had become so popular that it needed dynamism. In order to provide it, a programming language for the web was needed. So eyes naturally turned to what was then the fashionable language that was revolutionizing everything, Java.

While Java was shining for its cross-platform capabilities at that time, its virtual machine was still far from the level of optimization it has today. Netscape even tried to write, not long after, a 100% Java browser called *Javagator*, but it was too slow.

> *Java is to JavaScript what Car is to Carpet.*
>
> *— Chris Heilmann, german developer evangelist*

Plan B was to hire Brendan Eich to create a language that resembled Java as soon as possible but was much smaller and faster.

It would not yet be called *Javascript*. It was baptized as *Mocha*. It was later renamed *LiveScript* and finally, in a marketing move, agreed with Sun Microsystems, the creators of *Java*, they renamed it *JavaScript*.

Twenty-five years later, novice programmers worldwide are still wondering why Javascript has Java in its name if they have nothing technically to do with each other. And the answer can be summed up in one word: *marketing*.

PROGRAMMING AT THE EDGE OF THE LAW

At the turn of the century, the industry dictated where and how consumers were allowed to play their DVDs. A DVD purchased in the United States was not playable in Italy, and not only that, but a DVD could not be played on devices that were not certified. This was achieved by encrypting the DVDs' contents with a CSS (*content scrambling* system).

CSS left out GNU/Linux, the hackers' favorite operating system, as there was no certified player. However, programmers from all over the world accepted the challenge of trying to make it possible to play DVDs on Linux, even if this meant skipping the protection system created by the powerful film industry.

A group of three programmers, formed by the 16-year-old Norwegian Jon Lech Johansen (also known as *DVD John*) and two other programmers of whom we still do not know their identity, programmed *DeCSS*, a software capable of bypassing the protections of

DVDs, allowing playback on GNU/Linux. The problem was that, coincidentally or not, it also allows the copying of DVDs, a fact that the industry did not like at all.

Jon was persecuted in Norway, where he was acquitted in multiple appeals. As the legal battle was not going to end like this, in the United States, the web pages that distributed the DeCSS code were sued. The plaintiffs said the code went against the DMCA (*Digital Millennium Copyright Act*), while the advocates framed the code within free speech, as it had been done successfully before. However, the judge in the case ruled that freedom of expression does not protect code that can be compiled into an executable.

Between surprise and spite, the developer community found creative forms of protest using the backdoor the judge had left open with *not being able to be compiled into an executable*. They created dozens of ways to legally distribute the code, such as T-shirts, math descriptions, Japanese poetry, dramatic readings, and even music coded in MIDI format. The media coverage of the case and the creative solutions to distribute the code of DeCSS remain in the popular imagination of all those who lived at the beginning of the century.

Interestingly, thanks to DeCSS allowing scrutiny of the protection system, a way to bypass protection using brute force was discovered, thus opening the door for a modern computer to bypass protection in just a few seconds.

DEMOSCENE

In the early '80s, Europe was in the so-called golden age of the 8-bit. At that time, the IBM PC had not yet fully reached most homes due to its price and being oriented almost exclusively to *serious* matters.

In the homes reigned various computers from different manufacturers but with relatively similar characteristics. These computers were used for spreadsheets, word processors, small databases, and without a doubt, gaming.

Since the programs were distributed on discs and cassettes, as far as games were concerned, there was a whole black market in the streets, schools, and playgrounds. As a result, game developers were forced to create copy protection systems (see anti-copying systems, 48), which led to pirates creating cracks against those anti-copy systems.

On the street, creating cracks was something very prestigious. A pirate would surely leave his pseudonym visible for a quick instant in a game in the same way that a graffiti artist would sign his work.

Those names visible for an instant would end up becoming images and being called *Crack intros* or *cracktros*. The first known crack intro was from a group from Berlin called the *Berlin Cracking Service*, who put an image of the Berlin flag when loading the game *Pitfall II: Lost Caverns*.

Over time, all the hacking groups animated and introduced sound effects into their cracktros. Finally, it reached the point that the prestige of the hacking group was intimately related to the quality of its cracktro.

Because of the competition between the groups in search of that prestige, the cracktros improved and improved until for a combination of reasons, among which were included that piracy was increasingly persecuted and that cracktos were often seen as more fun to do than a crack in itself, cracktros stopped serving as an introduction to pirated games to become an art in itself.

That's how the demoscene was born. A culture of creating demos that show a group's technical and artistic skills to make the most of the available hardware, which was very limited at the time, by any trick available.

The scene grew and grew, and since phone calls were still expensive in Europe and the Internet and their predecessors were not particularly widespread, demo parties were created to learn and compete together.

In the early 90s, PCs finally began to replace the classic 8-bit computers. The power of these computers was much higher, effectively making the art of taking advantage of the hardware less critical. Also, since the arrival of Windows did not allow direct access to the hardware, it was practically impossible. The advent of 3D acceleration and the fact that self-imposed limits for competing, such as creating demos limited to 64 Kilobytes, ceased to make sense, led to the demoscene's fading.

However, the demoscene has not entirely disappeared. There are still very loyal followers. But even if it had, its influence already guarantees it a place in history. For example, the video game studios Remedy Entertainment, known for creating Max Paine, were founded by the renowned demoscene group Future Crew and Jaakko Iisalo, the creator of Angry Birds, was a well-known demoscener in the '90s.

GAME
OVER

TABLE OF CONTENTS

ACKNOWLEDGEMENTS

The author would like to thank the following individuals and organizations for the permission to reproduce the following resources:

Jaime Cobos for pixelated Víctor in page 4.

Dirk Oppelt from **cpu-collection.de** CPU picture in page 9.

Daniel Gordon, Martyn Johnson and **Quentin Stafford-Fraser** for the coffee maker picture in page 9. **Quentin Stafford-Fraser** for the last picture of the webcam in page 10.

Bill Bertram for Commodore 64 picture in page 11.

Steve Heal for Mitch's signature in page 11.

Adam Jenkins for the Osborne I picture in page 14 and the Apple II Plus picture in page 17.

André Karwath for the IBM Thinkpad picture of page 18.

JericoDelayah (Wikipedia username) for the Richard Stallman picture in page 20.

Bug de l'an 2000 (Wikipedia username) for l'école centrale de Nantes picture in page 21.

Scott Stilphen from **ataricompendium.com** for the letter to Atari in page 29.

Dota 2 The International (flickr user) for Gabe's picture in page 45.

Chiaerae (Wikipedia username) for the deep web iceberg metaphor in page 65.

Regarding the picture of John von Neumann in page 84. This image comes from Los Alamos National Laboratory, a national laboratory privately operated under contract from the United States Department of Energy by Los Alamos National Security. Unless otherwise indicated, this information has been authored by an employee or employees of the Los Alamos National Security, LLC (LANS), operator of the Los Alamos National Laboratory under Contract No. DE-

AC52-06NA25396 with the U.S. Department of Energy. The U.S. Government has rights to use, reproduce, and distribute this information. The public may copy and use this information without charge, provided that this Notice and any statement of authorship are reproduced on all copies. Neither the Government nor LANS makes any warranty, express or implied, or assumes any liability or responsibility for the use of this information.

The **Science Museum Group** for the Babbage's Analytical Engine in page 75.

Wolfgang Hunscher, Dortmund for the picture of Konrad Zuse in page 78.

SRI International for the Douglas Engelbart picture in page 86.

Ben Lowe for the picture of Brian Kernighan in page 90.

Woodcutter Manero for cursors font and **Khurasan** for Lets Coffee.

The software and the logos appearing in the screenshots in pages 24, 25, 29, 41, 42, 43, 46 and 50 are not copyright of the author but of their respective owners.

The covers, snippets and the logos appearing in the magazines and other paper media captures in pages 30, 47, 48, 50, 51, 91 and 93 are not copyright of the author but of their respective owners.